The Beautiful Disciplines

By the same author:

The Ideas Factory

The Think Tank

500 Prayers for Young People

The Beautiful Disciplines

Helping young people to develop
their spiritual roots

Martin Saunders

MONARCH
BOOKS

Oxford, UK & Grand Rapids, Michigan, USA

First published in the UK in 2011 by Monarch Books
(a publishing imprint of Lion Hudson plc),
Wilkinson House, Jordan Hill Road, Oxford OX2 8DR, England.
Tel: +44 (0)1865 302750 Fax: +44 (0)1865 302757
Email: monarch@lionhudson.com
www.lionhudson.com

ISBN 978 0 85721 055 5 (print)
ISBN 978 0 85721 247 4 (epub)
ISBN 978 0 85721 246 7 (Kindle)
ISBN 978 0 85721 248 1 (PDF)

Distributed by:
UK: Marston Book Services, PO Box 269, Abingdon, Oxon, OX14 4YN
USA: Kregel Publications, PO Box 2607, Grand Rapids, Michigan 49501

The text paper used in this book has been made from wood independently certified as having come from sustainable forests.

British Library Cataloguing Data
A catalogue record for this book is available from the British Library.

Printed and bound in Malta by Gutenberg Press.

Dedication

For my guinea pigs at St Mary's Reigate:

Josh Andrew, Justin Ball, Will Dyer, Dan Girdler,

David Guest, Sam Johnson, Dan Sterry and Adam Strode

Contents

Acknowledgments

Huge thanks to Tony Collins, Simon Cox and Jenny Ward at Monarch for their grace in handling a sometimes indisciplined writer, and for their persistent belief that this book needed to happen.

Thanks also to Helen Crawford, Laura Haddow, Sean Skinner, and everyone at *Youthwork* magazine who contributed ideas and encouragement when they were most needed.

Foreword

We live in a culture that is largely consumerist, individualistic, instant, celebrity-driven and, above all, superficial. Just as Israel were regularly prone to worship the idols of the culture around them, so it is with much of the church today. We want Jesus on the cheap. He is another accessory, another self-help tool, another spiritual gadget to make life easier. He is there for our convenience, like shopping on Amazon. Just one click and our spiritual, emotional and even material needs will be met. Superficiality really is the curse of our age.

About thirty years ago I read a book that was truly life changing and (after the Bible) remains my favourite. *Celebration of Discipline* by Richard Foster was a breath of spiritual fresh air. Richard went back to the classic spiritual disciplines of the church and brought them to life for people like me. They are the doorway to freedom, the signposts to a deeper life. I have been recommending *Celebration of Discipline* for nineteen years at Soul Survivor and Momentum festivals. Many have bought copies. To my dismay, many reported that they never got to the end. It wasn't written in their language, many found it a little hard going. That is why I am delighted to see *The Beautiful Disciplines* by Martin Saunders. This follows in the great tradition of the contemplative writings that have so inspired and renewed the Church through the years. Yet Martin writes in a way that is accessible to today's generation. He beautifully unblocks the ancient wells in a style that communicates, is inclusive, warm, fun and full of passion. Just like the man himself. Yet the contents are dynamite. Putting the truths and principles of this book into practice will revolutionise your life. The disciplines are not easy. However, they are beautiful because they lead you to Jesus. We are a church that needs to be discipled. Many are slightly dissatisfied with their walk with God because they have not been told what is possible. This book proclaims loud and clear that we can go deeper and shows us how.

I honestly believe *The Beautiful Disciplines* is a vital resource for anyone who wants to take seriously Jesus' command and invitation to "follow me". My hope and prayer is that it will result in many deep, passionate, humble and Christ-like followers of Jesus who, through their lives as well as their words, will change their world.

I commend it to you.

Mike Pilavachi
September 2011.

Introduction

Silence. Restraint.
Contemplation.

If we're entirely honest, these are not words that often find their way into the vocabulary of your average young person. Or, indeed, your average *older* person. In today's restless world, where devices in our pocket keep us entirely and unendingly connected, where microwave meals start to become frustrating once they pass the four-minute mark, where a prominent maxim for living is "Get rich or die tryin'", we don't have a lot of time for stillness. In a society that aims to shape people not into citizens but into consumers, where the true mark of a successful education is the production of a financially independent young spender, what place is there for a message of restraint? And, in an age in which Google has made us entry-level experts in everything, what need do we have for study?

On the one hand, then, you could be about to read one of the least relevant books ever written. Because this is a book about discipline, for the most part involving all the areas of the self that modern life suggests are redundant. In fact, it's worse than that; this is a book about *Spiritual Disciplines*: meaning that we're looking at those redundant areas through a lens – Christianity – that much of our "progressive" society has left behind. And in fact it gets even worse still. This is actually a book about using the ancient Christian Spiritual Disciplines with *teenagers*. It's about introducing ideas such as fasting and solitude to the most connected, most marketed-to generation there has even been. As tough sells go, it seems akin to asking your granddad to take up skateboarding and start listening to hip hop.

Or is it?

Is it instead possible that there is something in the Spiritual Disciplines for young people; that the ancient methods by which Christians have been drawing near to God for centuries might still have something profound to say to them? Is it even possible that by introducing them to concepts such as retreat, celebration and study, we might be able to unlock for them whole new areas of life and spirituality?

This book has been written out of a passionate belief that the Spiritual Disciplines are not just theoretically good for young people, but that they will be gasped in like oxygen when properly explained. As unlikely as it sounds, I believe that equipping young people with a practical understanding of a wide range of Disciplines will provide them with tangible ways of connecting with God, and enable them to grow significantly in their faith. I have seen young people fall in love with these ancient practices and, in so doing, fall more in love with God.

Brittle

The idea for this book came from countless conversations with youth workers and teenagers, out of which I drew one significant conclusion: modern Christian youth discipleship is producing brittle disciples. **That is to say, the work we do with young people in their childhood and adolescence does not seem to ensure that those individuals retain an active faith into adulthood.**

I write this as a volunteer youth worker who has helped to run groups and disciple teenagers for close to a decade. I am absolutely a part of the problem. In that role, I have seen some young people move on and grow in their faith: Sarah, who now works for a major evangelistic organization and is full of passion to pass on her faith to the next generation; Jamie, who completely turned his life around and went on a direct route from being an angry, out-of-control teenager to becoming a trainee youth worker himself. We all have our success stories.

We also all have other stories (names changed here): Gemma, who as an attractive and popular seventeen-year-old tried so hard to go against the flow, but one day decided to choose a lifestyle of nightclubs and older men, and never came back; Tom, who left for university as a worship leader and Bible teacher, and came back at half-term with a permanent hangover and a total lack of interest in church. Perhaps because God has revealed some of His heart to us, these stories grieve us the most. It's those young people whom we lie awake thinking about, wondering whether we could have done more.

In one sense that's the wrong question, and when I ask it at least, it betrays in me a sense that I am in control. For youth workers, it is so easy to begin to believe – sometimes without even realizing that we do – that it's all about us. That the eternal destiny of these young people is entirely in our hands. "No-one comes to the Father except through me," says Jesus in John 14:6, but often we add our own names into that equation. Like Oskar Schindler at the end of *Schindler's List*, we beat ourselves up that "we could have saved one more…" Ultimately, we need to remember that salvation, and the long-term relationship between God and another individual, is not our responsibility. Just because Tom and Gemma have turned their backs on God and church, it doesn't mean that God has given up on them.

As youth workers, then, our job is to join in with what God is already doing in the world: lending a hand where He is already active, where His plans are well under way. Our job, according to Jesus in Matthew 28, is to "go and make disciples", but we don't do this in a vacuum – we do it with God standing beside us. Discipleship can perhaps be defined as properly introducing someone to God. That doesn't mean simply leading them to the door of faith, knocking on it and then running away, but explaining something of the person of God to them, and equipping them with the tools to meet with Him.

Is that what your discipleship looks like? If I'm honest, it isn't always an accurate definition of mine. If I'm not careful, my version of youth discipleship can often mean I'm trying to turn young people into miniature versions of myself, not of Christ. And perhaps that's unavoidable sometimes: it's only right after all that we lead by example; it's a very positive thing to share something of our lives with the young people we disciple. Yet if my investment in their faith development is limited to doing "stuff together" – reading, praying, projects on justice and evangelism – what happens when I am taken out of the equation?

There is a common problem in youth ministry to do with the "celebrity" youth pastor.[1] It's an uncomfortable truth to accept, but many youth ministries are built more around the charisma and personality of their leader than they are around a communal love of God. In almost all cases this isn't intentional, but merely

---

1   For more on this, see Dave Wright's article "Me-Centred Ministry" in the September 2008 issue of *Youthwork* magazine.

a natural side effect of having an engaging and likeable youth worker in the driving seat (and who wouldn't want that?). The concern isn't necessarily the charismatic leader, however, but whether, alongside the exciting, fun, up-front aspects of their work, they are also equipping their young people with the tools to develop a faith that endures beyond their input. Because, of course, the problem with personality-driven youth work doesn't become apparent until the youth worker leaves (or, unfortunately, suffers a moral lapse). That's when youth groups that have seen hundreds coming through their doors can suddenly melt into nothing. And if our youth work feeds the consumerist paradigm, why should we be in the least bit surprised? Youth-worker-centred youth work of any kind is like putting the bass player on lead vocals: ultimately, young people are going to stop listening to the music.

Just as truly great preaching leaves a congregation in awe of God rather than of the preacher, good Christian youth work creates disciples who are increasingly in touch with God – and not through the middleman of a youth worker. Our aim should be to encourage direct connections.

This book aims to resource you, the youth worker, to equip young people with the tools to build those direct connections with God. It hinges on the idea that the Spiritual Disciplines, which we'll define in a moment, contain the power to strengthen and reinforce brittle young disciples, and so ensure that their faith endures the leaps, pitfalls and changes of season that lie on the path to adulthood. If that's a bold claim, then it is made with this caveat: the Disciplines themselves are not magic formulae; each simply draws the individual or community practising it closer to God. It is He who does all the strengthening, reinforcing and deepening of relationship; it is He who changes hearts.

What are the Disciplines?

There is no hidden chapter in some dark corner of the Old Testament entitled "Hezekiah's list of Spiritual Disciplines". In fact, a definitive list of the Disciplines simply doesn't exist. They are the activities of the spiritual life – not just the inner life, but a life lived in constant communion with God. In his 1953 book *Thoughts in Solitude*, Catholic writer Thomas Merton says, "The spiritual life is first of all a life. It is not merely something to be known and studied, it is to be lived." The Disciplines are meant not just to be understood, but experienced.

Theologian Dallas Willard defines the Spiritual Disciplines as "what you do to modify your inner person… an activity in my power that enables me to accomplish what I can't do by direct effort".[2] He seems to be suggesting that, by choosing to engage with God through the Disciplines, we can achieve a higher state of being – that is to say, a closer state to the one God intends for us. The Spiritual Disciplines lie at the core of the ancient mystic tradition of the Christian faith. They were practised and propounded by the great saints and heroes of the faith, men and women such as Augustine, Patrick and Theresa. As the church grew and developed, devotion to these practices created a constant connection to God that fuelled evangelism and growth. The

---

2   Teaching CD: *The Great Omission: Reclaiming Jesus's Essential Teachings on Discipleship*, Hovel Audio, 2007.

Disciplines practised ranged from those with an inward focus, such as prayer, to those with an outward or communal focus. There are some ancient spiritual practices that are often included in a wider list of Disciplines, which have very noble intentions and focus us wholly on God, but are not described in the Bible itself. Some people – many of them quite wise – have expressed concern and discomfort about some of these practices, suggesting that they stray away from biblically-modelled spirituality and into the territory of the New Age. To err on the side of caution, and to remove any unwanted stumbling block for those who hold such concerns, I have compiled a list of Disciplines with one important qualifying rule: they are each clearly practised and advocated in Scripture.

My humble suggestion, and the reason for this book, is that often in our work with young people we sell them short when we provide them with the tools to enjoy a relationship with God. We tell them about prayer (although perhaps only a quite limited view of it); we teach them to read the Bible. But there are so many other ways of reaching out to and connecting with God – time-honoured, biblical and proven methods that are part of the history of our faith. As I said right at the beginning, we may sometimes find it hard to believe that today's young people, born into this fast-paced digital culture, could ever make sense of the Disciplines, which, as the word suggests, all require a slowing down, a focusing of the mind, a concentration of will. Yet I know this isn't true; more than that, I have found from experience that young people can learn to love and cherish them. Why? Because the Disciplines lead them to God.

How does this book work?

This is principally a resource book, although all being well quite a holistically minded one. We all recognize that every youth group, every young person even, is a slightly different context from the next. What works with the midweek Bible study group at St Cuthbert's[3] will not, without some serious adaptation, work in the God slot at an open youth club. I do believe, however, that all the subjects and themes covered in this resource have something to offer to all young people – it's all about how you, the youth leader, present them. To help you, then, I've set out to make this book as adaptable as possible. Each of the Disciplines covered is presented with an introduction to help you engage with it first. Then in each chapter, you get three resources, all adaptable and all pitched slightly differently.

The **First Steps** resources are basically adaptable discussion starters, based on the format I've used in my previous books *The Ideas Factory* and *The Think Tank*. They take the form of a story (see those books for my thoughts on the power of using story with young people), which introduces a theme, followed by several banks of questions designed to get young people talking. In the context of the other resources, these are perhaps best suited to young people who are warm to the idea of faith, but may not have yet made a commitment to follow Christ. These

---

3 Apologies to all the youth workers who actually *do* work for a St Cuthbert's. You guys are always the butt of the joke. Cuthbert is a hero of the faith, and we should not poke fun at his name, any more than we should chuckle at the existence of churches called New International Fellowship of the Redeemed River of Fire Ministries. (Apologies also if you're the youth worker at New International Fellowship of the Redeemed River of Fire Ministries...)

discussion starters assume no prior knowledge on the part of their participants, and could therefore also be tailored for use in school – perhaps in an RE lesson or an assembly. If possible, you might like to try to give at least half an hour to running one of these resources with young people, but, of course, often you won't have that luxury.

The **Adaptable Meeting Guides** are the heart of the book, and can be used as stand-alone lesson plans that address a particular Spiritual Discipline, or as a term-long course (see notes on running *The Beautiful Disciplines* as a course, below). Although I have included notes for customizing them for use with unchurched young people, they are generally pitched at young people with some level of Christian faith. The guides, based on the format used in *Youthwork* magazine, assist you in leading young people on a journey around a subject, through games, activities, discussion, Bible study, and, of course, engagement with the Disciplines. I have included approximate timings for each element of the sessions – of course, depending on the engagement and enthusiasm of your group, these may become wildly inaccurate in practice! However, ideally you will want to allow at least an hour to run each of these sessions, and in an hour you're highly unlikely to get through all the material. My suggestion is always that you take some time ahead of the meeting to cherry-pick the best and most relevant parts of the guide, look at **Adapting the Material** and make sure the session is really going to work in your context.

Going Deeper resources provide you with some practical extra activities to continue your exploration of the Disciplines with young people. They can be added into one of the meeting guides, used as a follow-up, or perhaps saved for an opportune moment of recap – in your usual context, at a residential weekend away, or at a camp or festival. Whereas the activities included in the meeting guides are mainly intended to encourage corporate engagement with the Disciplines, many of the Going Deeper activities encourage personal reflection and response. The ultimate aim of this book is to help you to help young people to develop a deeper connection with God through these powerful ancient tools, and so these more "advanced" ideas are designed for them to take away and incorporate into their own devotional time. The amount of time you might need to allocate to these ideas will vary quite a bit – again, it's a good idea to plan and adapt the resource in advance of your meeting with the young people.

Notes on running *The Beautiful Disciplines* as a course

The resources in this book may lend themselves well to being used as a course. Using the Adaptable Meeting Guides, you can pick and choose the subjects you want to cover, and construct a six-, eight-, or even eleven-week course. You may want to combine certain Disciplines (for instance, Submission and Service), or leave some out altogether. In my humble opinion, it is in running a term-long series on these practices that you will see the greatest impact on your group. In working to combat the kind of brittleness I described earlier, we need to help young people to create a whole range of ways in which they relate to

God. Dedicating a term or other lengthy period to looking at the Disciplines will underline how important you believe them to be, and give young people time and space to work out which of these practices will be helpful in shaping their own spiritual life.

I would also suggest that you start your series with an introductory session, explaining the Disciplines and their application to life. This will help you to gauge interest and enthusiasm for these topics, and also to conduct a simple "discipleship audit", which will allow the group to articulate their own perceptions of their spiritual life. If you have run a course or series of sessions, you may want to consider running this activity again during or after your final session.

To help you with all this, I have included a "Week Zero" meeting guide resource, introducing the series and the audit, for which you will find a simple photocopiable questionnaire at the back of the book (Appendix i). All the meeting guides include some small-group work, so, depending on the size and context of your group, you may want to establish fixed groups at the start of the term, which remain together for the whole course. You don't need to be tied to this – the groups might need shuffling around for one reason or another – but it could help some personality types to feel more relaxed if they know whom they'll be relating to each week.

If you are running the course over an entire term, you may even want to consider building in a residential weekend away somewhere in the middle. How might your group cope with going away together on a guided retreat? Again, this might seem quite ambitious, but I have constantly been surprised by the willingness of young people to put down their ever-connected lifestyle in the search for something tangibly spiritual.

The resources could also be used as a kind of course, or at least as shorter discussion session subjects for a season of meetings. If you are using them in an open youth club, Christian Union or other similar context, you could see this as an opportunity to open up the expectations of young people – Christian or otherwise – to the available depths of the Christian life. My hunch is that most people who don't have a faith have no idea of the range of ways in which, for hundreds of years, God's people have been engaging with Him.

My great hope for these resources is that they will encourage young people to go much deeper with God, in ways that both bring their faith alive and create a concrete foundation for a life with Him. The resources are only one part of the equation, however, and the lesser part at that. Their success depends much more on your ability to adapt them for the specific young people with whom you work, and on the extraordinary, mysterious, powerful and miraculous God to whom you are introducing them. So, while it might sound obvious, do spend time praying for the divine and unexpected spark of God in each of these meetings, that He would take our words and do something remarkable with them in the lives of young people.

On that note, it is important that we practise what we preach. Young people can smell inauthenticity a mile off. I urge and encourage you to investigate and practise the Disciplines yourself. Before you attempt to run a session, try to take some time to stop, to connect with God, to "play" in the Disciplines. Read my introductions by all means, but see them as the first word on each subject, not the last. I am a resource writer, not an expert, and there are many fantastic books on the subject which make my thoughts look like the ramblings of a pre-schooler. In particular I recommend:

Celebration of Discipline – The Path to Spiritual Growth by Richard Foster (Hodder & Stoughton, revised ed. 1989).

The Spirit of the Disciplines – Understanding How God Changes Lives by Dallas Willard (HarperCollins, 1991).

The Life You've Always Wanted by John Ortberg (Zondervan, revised ed. 2002).

Week Zero

Introducing the Spiritual Disciplines

The adaptable meeting guide

Meeting aim: To introduce the Spiritual Disciplines to young people, and explode their ideas of the ways in which we can connect with God. This is primarily intended as an introduction to running *The Beautiful Disciplines* as a course.

Before you start: Make sure you have a good grasp of the subject. I would strongly recommend that you read or revisit Richard Foster's landmark book *Celebration of Discipline*. For the session you will need: an army drill sergeant (or impersonator thereof); copies of the Discipleship Audit (see Appendix i); a copy of the list of Spiritual Disciplines and definitions for each group; colourful pens for each group.

Drill
(10–15 minutes)

Take the group into a fairly open space, such as a hall, if you are able to. Ask them to line up against a wall and explain that, as part of a new drive to improve behaviour, you have recruited a local army drill sergeant to drum some discipline into them. Bring in the real thing if possible, or at least an actor who is going to take the job very seriously; do not let on that this is all a joke. Get the "instructor" to teach the group some basic drill moves (Attention! Stand at ease! That sort of thing…), and then have him/her put it all together into a short routine. Once the group has performed it, allow the "instructor" the pleasure of revealing that this isn't for real after all – but don't let it slip until that point. Explain to the group that over the coming weeks we are going to be exploring discipline together, although not quite like this!

Getting to know you
(10 minutes)

Divide into small groups of six to eight if possible (it may be that these are pre-determined groups which will be staying together for the whole of the course). If you can, try to make the groups varied, so that groups of friends aren't all placed together. Then ask the members of each group to introduce themselves to one another, and then answer this question:

• How self-disciplined are you? Are you the sort of person who thrives on making and following rules for yourself, or are you wildly undisciplined, disorganized, always running late?

Give the groups some time to discuss this – especially if the conversation appears to be flowing. If it doesn't, you could prompt groups with further questions:

- *How "tidy" is your life?*

- *How good or bad are you at finishing what you've started?*

- *How important do you think it is to be organized, on time, and up to date?*

Draw the discussions to a close by explaining that self-discipline is a spiritual matter. The Bible says that "Like a city whose walls are broken down is a man who lacks self-control" (Proverbs 25:28); the whole Bible is littered with references to it (the list of fruits of the Spirit in Galatians 5 is a great in-context example). Self-discipline is crucial if we're going to live lives that are consistent for God – and if we are going to attempt to regularly connect with Him.

From self-discipline to spiritual disciplines (10 minutes)

Explain: this session is all about exploring the ancient Christian tradition of the Spiritual Disciplines. They were famously practised by saints and heroes of the faith, men and women who were instrumental in the development of Christianity from a group of rebels and radicals into a global religion followed by billions. They have their root, however, in the Bible, and in the example of Jesus Himself. Read Luke 5:12–16 (Jesus heals a man with leprosy). Ask the group as a whole if they find anything strange about verses 14–16. In particular:

- Why does Jesus ask him not to tell anyone?

- What would you have done in that man's situation? Would you have remained quiet?

- Why does Jesus retreat to be by Himself, just at the moment when crowds are surging to be near Him? What does this teach us, if we are supposed to follow Jesus' example?

Make sure this point is shared: Jesus Himself practised Spiritual Discipline – and in this one verse (verse 16) we see the very core of the Disciplines in action – Jesus has withdrawn to a place of solitude, and is spending time alone with God. In the same way, the Spiritual Disciplines are designed to provide an opportunity for God to work in our lives.

The unspiritual disciplines (10 minutes)

Give each group a large piece of paper (at least A3) and, in the middle, include the following list of the Spiritual Disciplines (which are explored in the resources in this book). Next to each one, you might wish to add a few words of explanation, depending on how much your group is likely to understand.

Prayer

Study (mainly of the Bible)

Fasting

Meditation

Simplicity

Solitude

Submission

Service

Worship

Celebration

Run through the headings to make sure everyone in the room understands what they mean. Now ask the groups to imagine what the absolute opposite to each might be. So, for instance, the opposite of fasting might be eating an extra meal each day, or indulging in twenty-four hours of non-stop gluttony! Ask them to use coloured pens to annotate the list with their opposites. As they do so, suggest that they discuss what the impact of these opposite Disciplines might be if they were applied to our lives.

Have the groups feed back their funniest, most poignant or interesting "unSpiritual Disciplines". Now ask: does your life right now look more like the original list, or the new one?! Which list do you think would be a better template for living?

God audit
(15 minutes)

Our first moment of alone time (and there are plenty more to come). Give each member of your group a copy of the Discipleship Audit (see Appendix i), and a pen to complete it with. Stress that this is not for anyone else's eyes – it isn't going to be collected. Explain that this is simply a tool to help them to understand for themselves the nature of their relationship with God, and their engagement with each of the Spiritual Disciplines.

Suggest they find a quiet space, away from their friends, where they can complete the form. Try to create an atmosphere of silence, or, if this is unrealistic in your context, play some instrumental music to encourage people not to talk. Before they start, ask them to spend just a few moments on their own (not looking at the form), turning their thoughts and attention to God. Give them ten minutes to complete the form, then ask them to put it somewhere safe – you will look at it again at the end of the course.

Wrap-up
(5 minutes)

Draw the various ideas in the session together. Over the next few weeks, we're going to be looking at the different tools available that can help us to get closer to God – and we can see how practising them will both improve our relationship with Him and emulate the way Jesus behaved when He was on earth. In the weeks to come we should ask God to give us the gift of self-discipline, as we seek to become more disciplined in our pursuit of Him.

Ask one of the group or leaders to close with a prayer, asking God to reveal Himself and draw each of you closer to Him over the coming weeks.

ADAPTING THE MATERIAL

For older groups… You may not get away with the drill sergeant without letting them in on the joke beforehand.

For younger groups… Use the "Getting to know you" section simply to introduce everyone, and perhaps to talk about what it means practically to be a Christian. Does that mean your life looks different? How do you spend your time differently as a result?

For churchgoing young people… Perhaps introduce the section looking at the individual Disciplines by asking – how many do you practise already? Which do you find easier or more difficult?

For unchurched young people… This session is aimed at young people who have a Christian faith already. However, the Spiritual Disciplines are a brilliant way to introduce someone to God for the first time. The First Steps resources, found in each chapter of this book, may be a better place to start.

Part One:
THE CORE

The Inward Disciplines

Week One

Engage: The Discipline of Prayer

"Be joyful always; pray continually; give thanks in all circumstances, for this is God's will for you in Christ Jesus."

1 Thessalonians 5:16–18

How do you really see prayer? As divine poetry, connecting you via a hotline to the Almighty? As a religious duty-cum-self-help mechanism that allows you to organize your thoughts? For most of us, the reality is somewhere in between these two extremes.

I have always disliked what some people call "open prayer". Sitting in a circle of Christians, hands fixed to the sides of my head as if I'm trying to cover up a superglue accident, I often think this is one of the least spiritual places I can find myself. Here is an honest description of what I do in such a meeting. First, I listen to the inevitable list of prayer requests, and select one that a) I completely understand, and b) doesn't sound too difficult to pray for. Then, as voices begin to fill the silence, I start work on my masterpiece: a poetic form of words that would have T. S. Eliot on his feet applauding. I work out my first line, then my second. Then I try to come up with some sort of sound bite for the middle part that will make everyone else in the circle make an affirming "hmm" noise, as if someone has just switched on seven food mixers. Then I make sure I know how I'm going to land, for fear of ending with one of those awful fudgy forms of words like "for the Father Jesus Christ's holy sake". Then I wait for a gap, and launch into my dramatized poetry reading. And, of course, I have listened to and engaged with none of the other prayers.

Is that what prayer is about? Of course not – in fact, in Matthew 6:5–8, Jesus suggests that prayer should take place in an inner room with the door closed. It's the very opposite of the hideously dysfunctional situation I've just described, and a helpful counter to the act of "horizontal prayer", which is more for the benefit of the people you're praying with than the God you're supposed to be praying to.

Prayer because I ought to...

There is a scene in Shakespeare's *Hamlet* in which the hero decides to kill off his no-good father, the king, but when he arrives to do the deed he finds him at prayer. Concerned that by killing him during prayer he'll send him to heaven (rather than the hell Hamlet thinks he deserves), he stands down. But, after he has walked away, the king makes an admission: "My words fly up; my thoughts remain below: Words without thoughts never to heaven go" (*Hamlet*, Act 3, Scene 3, 99–100).

While this isn't biblical theology, it's a good illustration of the limitations of "religious" prayers. If we're praying out of a sense of duty, then we're praying for the wrong reasons. Prayer is about relationship, not obligation. In fact there are a whole host of ways in which we can find ourselves praying for the wrong reason. Praying for the sake of our own reassurance, like chanting a self-help mantra; praying so others will hear our words; praying out of guilt or duty. None of this is what prayer is about – yet, when I consider my own prayers, so many of these motivators can be present.

Corporate or individual?

What's really interesting about Jesus' words in Matthew 6 is that they suggest that prayer is an activity for individuals, not communities. Going into a room and closing the door is a rather antisocial antithesis of much of the prayer that goes on among Christians. And this isn't a verse out of context: again and again in the Bible, we see prayer described as an individual, one-on-one activity. Throughout His ministry, and culminating in Gethsemane, Jesus retires to be by Himself to pray, and Paul repeatedly gives accounts of his own prayer life. There are a few examples in the New Testament that recommend communal prayer (e.g. Matthew 18:19), but overwhelmingly, it seems to me that prayer is intended largely as an inner discipline.

A common criticism of the modern church, and particularly the modern worship music movement, is that it turns Christianity into an individualistic faith when it is meant to be a corporate journey. The picture of the church in Acts 2, where the believers share all their possessions to ensure that no one goes without, is an indictment of the twenty-first-century Western church to which we have no answer. The description of God in John 1:1 shows a Trinity which itself lives in community. Contrary to many of the songs we sing, the Christian faith isn't about "me, me, me", but "us, us, us".

It's almost amusing, then, that in the context of an often-individualistic faith, prayer is one of the mechanisms by which we join together in community. It's as if we're holding the instructions the wrong way up: the biblical picture is one of a fully-functional community which divides only to spend time in personal prayer and devotion, yet often we act as a group of individuals who come together for meetings to pray!

"Pray continually"

So enough, then, about what prayer isn't. Time surely to ask: what *is* prayer? If we analyse the blueprint for prayer that Jesus lays out in Matthew 6, we find a lot of the subjects we should cover – confession, praise, thanksgiving, requests – but even that doesn't answer what prayer *is*. To answer that question, we need to look at Jesus' example and Paul's application.

In Luke 5:12–16 (a passage we'll return to several times), Jesus heals a man of leprosy. Then, as the word gets out about Him, and the crowds gather to celebrate Him, Jesus turns and runs in the opposite direction. And not just then – verse 16 says that "he *often* withdrew to lonely places and prayed". What does that tell us? That when things are happening around Him, when the heat is on, when everyone is running towards Him and saying "This is your moment", He retreats. He doesn't run head first into a crowd of adoring fans; He withdraws. And we read that He *often* did this. He withdraws to pray because, for Jesus, prayer is home. Not just when things are tough, as in the Garden of Gethsemane, but also when things are good. Prayer is Jesus' default setting; He continually returns to it because it is where He recharges and makes sense of things. We should surely follow His example.

In his letter to the Ephesians, Paul talks about prayer not as something we "go off and do", but as a constant state in which Christians should seek to find themselves. In chapter 6 he says: "… pray in the Spirit on *all occasions* with *all kinds* of prayers and requests. With this in mind, be alert and *always keep on praying* for all the saints" (verse 18, my italics). His language here isn't a coincidence, nor is he being emotive and over-the-top. He is suggesting that prayer (just as in the verse from 1 Thessalonians that begins this chapter) is an ongoing process. Changing our view of prayer from a series of moments to a continual journey is vital as we seek to engage with the Spiritual Disciplines.

Prayer as the foundation

Prayer is the Discipline that underpins all the others. It is the first and most important Spiritual Discipline, because it is the one that connects us directly to the heart of God. All the other Disciplines draw on it deeply; if the others are flavours of the spiritual life, then prayer is the life-sustaining water to which they are added. Prayer is therefore the first stop on our journey through the Disciplines. Before we can ask young people to throw themselves into a range of prayerful activities, we must first challenge and develop their notion of what prayer is and can be. And, of course, we should never grow tired of asserting that prayer isn't just about speaking words into thin air, but that it involves great and mysterious power. 1 John 5:14–15 says: "This is the confidence we have in approaching God: that if we ask anything according to his will, he hears us. And if we know that he hears us – whatever we ask – we know that we have what we asked of him."

Prayer is home. Prayer is continuous. Prayer is power. How might truly understanding these truths about prayer transform the way young people view their relationship with God?

Engage: Resources

First steps – The discussion starter

THE 100-YEAR PRAYER MEETING

Though born into German royalty, eighteenth-century Count Nikolaus Ludwig von Zinzendorf did not go down in history as a famous aristocrat. Instead, he was known as a man who, propelled by his Christian faith, cared for the poor and opened up his palatial property to refugees. The first ten arrived in 1722, and just three years later there were almost a hundred living on the site. He named the community that was forming there "Herrnhut", meaning "the Lord's Watchful Care", and saw it grow further, to almost 300, by the end of 1726. By then it had become a small town, run entirely on Christian principles – like a seven-day church where everything was shared and no one went hungry. The refugees brought and shared crafts and skills; these once-homeless people had begun to create a sustainable life for themselves, because Zinzendorf did not turn them away.

Even this was not the most remarkable part of Zinzendorf's story. After divisions and fighting began to break out in the Count's community, he organized the people into a sort of rota of prayer, so that at every hour of every day at least someone was praying. At the end of each hour, the baton would be passed to the next person to pray for one hour more. All day long, all night long. For a week, then a month, then a year. Every moment, of every hour, there was always someone praying in Herrnhut. This continuous prayer went on, uninterrupted, for a hundred years. During that time the community became the centre point of a revival in the European church, and sent more than 300 people off as missionaries around the world. They arrived as homeless peasants; they left as ministers on a mission. All because Zinzendorf opened the door to them, and taught them how to pray.

Opening up

Read the story above, then ask the following questions:

- Do you believe that the prayer meeting really continued uninterrupted for 100 years? Why?

- How do you think this small community kept the momentum going for so long?

- What does Zinzendorf's story make you think about prayer?

Digging deeper

- Why do people pray? What are some of the different reasons?

- What is prayer – if you had to describe it to someone who had never heard the word, how would you define it?

- What do you think happens when we pray? Are there some kinds of prayer, or people praying them, that you think might be more or less likely to be "heard"?

Taking it to the word

Read 1 Thessalonians 5:16–18

- Why do you think the things listed here are "God's will for us"?

- The words "all", "always" and "continually" appear in these short verses – what does this tell us about prayer?

- What would it look like to "pray continually"? Could you imagine how that might be possible for you?

- Consider experimenting with prayer together. What different methods of communication – writing, drawing, speaking, etc. – could you use to pray? Feed back later – what happened as a result of your prayers?

The adaptable meeting guide

Meeting aim: To explore the Discipline of Prayer by giving the young people new ways to think about and practise direct communication with God. To help them to see prayer not as a series of moments with God, but as an ongoing conversation that lasts a lifetime.

Before you start: You will need flip-chart paper; black pens – two to three per group (or at least lots of the same colour); highlighter pens – one or two per group; stopwatch; small chocolate prizes; Bibles; paper and envelopes.[4]

Just a minute
(10 minutes)

Begin the session by playing the classic radio game *Just a Minute*. You can do this either in small groups or, preferably, all together. Explain that there are prizes on offer for anyone who can talk to the group for one minute on a subject of their choosing. The twist is that, if they hesitate or repeat themselves, they lose the game and have to stop. It's harder than you might think, so call for a volunteer and time all your contestants with a stopwatch. If anyone gets to a minute without hesitation or repetition, give them a prize; if none of your volunteers make it that far, award prizes to those who managed to speak for the longest.

---

4 Further reading: A great book on helping young people to pray is *Helping Teenagers to Pray* (also known as *Downtime*) by Mark Yaconelli (SPCK, 2009).

Hard prayer
(10 minutes)

Divide into small groups, and ask them to discuss the following questions:

- *What is prayer?*

- *How and when do you tend to pray? What form do your prayers take?*

- *Do you find prayer, or making time to pray, difficult? Why or why not?*

Just another minute
(5 minutes)

Ask the group to find some space, and then explain that everyone is now going to attempt the "Just a Minute" activity – but this time we won't be talking about a favourite subject; we'll be praying. Depending on your group and on the young people involved, you may want to suggest that this happens in silence, in quiet with some music playing, or with everyone speaking loudly at the same time. Give them no time to think about what they will pray about, and give them no prayer requests or suggestions. Afterwards, get feedback from the whole group. Was that easy or difficult? Why? Ask those who also took part in the first game whether it was easier to pray non-stop for a minute, or to talk in front of an audience about a pet subject. Why do they think that is?

How many ways?
(15 minutes)

Give your groups large sheets of flip-chart paper and ask them to write down with the black pens as many methods of communication as they can think of: e.g. face to face, social networks, email, semaphore(!). If you encourage them to think a little laterally, they should be able to come up with dozens. You could award a small prize for the group that thinks of the most. Then, without getting them to "do" anything to the lists, ask how many ways they think there are of communicating with God. How many ways are there of praying? Ask them to go through their lists again, and, using the highlighter pens, to mark all the methods of communication that *could* theoretically be used to talk to God. Invite and allow plenty of discussion. God doesn't have an email address, but does that mean we can't use email to pray in some way? Does God hear our prayers if we write them down, draw them, or even post them onto our social media profiles?

We tend to think of prayer in quite a safe, limited way: perhaps just us in a room, or a few people in a group, saying words. But that's just one way of communicating – it's not what prayer is. Prayer is something else.

Continual prayer
(5 minutes)

In groups, ask the young people to look at 1 Thessalonians 5:16–18, then discuss:

- The words "all", "always" and "continually" appear in these short verses: what does this tell us about prayer?

- What would it look like to "pray continually"? Could you imagine how that might be possible for us?

Explain that prayer isn't just an activity that we check in and out of; it's an ongoing journey. Prayer is an attitude – meaning that we're always aware of God beside us in every conversation, every thought, every silence.

Prayer adventures (20 minutes)

Ask each group to look together at both of the following passages:

- 1 Kings 18:21–38

- Acts 12:5–10

Then ask them to discuss the following: who in each story was praying? What was the result? What do these stories tell us about prayer? Perhaps stories like this don't match up with our experience of prayer – yet if we believe they are true, then the same power is available to us. Give out pens, paper and envelopes, and get the groups to brainstorm some outrageous, adventurous things that they could pray for over the next week. The only rule is that they can't be safe – the sorts of things that could easily happen anyway! So it could mean:

- *Praying that a friend or parent might begin to ask questions about Jesus...*

- *Praying that God would speak to them powerfully and unmistakably...*

- *Praying that a major change will happen in your local school...*

After they've agreed on one adventurous prayer topic, invite them to write it down, put it in the envelope (don't seal it), and put it in their pocket. Then invite them to carry it around all week, constantly mentioning the prayer request to God. Next week, you may want to have a short time of feedback at the beginning of the session to find out what happened.

Recap: continuous and varied
(5 minutes)

Close the session by referring to the various means of communication that you brainstormed together. Either challenge your group to pick one new way to pray over the next week or use one or more of the Going Deeper activities to finish.

ADAPTING THE MATERIAL

For older groups... They might really enjoy the initial "Just a Minute" activity, so to allow more to take part you could hold this in small groups instead of all together.

For younger groups... Provide clues or prompts around the room, which may help them to think of different kinds of communication for the "How many ways" section.

For churchgoing young people... You could bring in more of the prayer activities from the Going Deeper section, and spread them throughout the session.

For unchurched young people... Pick just one Bible passage in the "Prayer Adventures" section – up to you which one – and make sure you have a leader in each group who is briefed and able to explain the story fully in context.

Going deeper: Follow-on activities

These ideas can be either added into the meeting guide, used as stand-alone activities, or suggested to young people for their own devotional time.

1. PRAYER PICTURES

Some of us find it difficult to put our deepest thoughts and most heartfelt emotions into words. Others just find we have a mental block when it comes to finding words to pray with. In either case, all we need to do is challenge the idea that prayer is about words. It isn't – it's simply about a heart-to-heart connection with God. This activity can be run with just a pen and paper, or a full-blown art and craft studio. The aim is simply to pray through the drawing of a picture.

Ask the young people to relax and spend a few moments in quiet, thinking about one of two things: either those events, people, or circumstances for which they are really thankful, or things in their lives that they would like to see changed or resolved in some way. After a few moments of silent contemplation, ask them to pick up their piece of paper, and – in an attitude of prayer – begin to create a picture. Give them as long as seems helpful; also allow them the option of annotating the drawing with text if they want to. At the end of the activity, do not ask them to share their prayer picture with the group, but encourage them to keep their picture and reflect on it again in the future.

2. LETTERS TO GOD

This is an activity that requires a bit of forward planning, but which I have personally seen reap incredible rewards. It works best if you can undertake the initial activity around six months before your group is planning to be at a camp, festival or residential break together – for reasons that will become clear.

Ask each member of your group to take a pen and paper (change this if your group doesn't "do" writing activities – maybe use a video camera instead), and write a "letter to God". They should include a few words about how they are feeling about their relationship with Him, some requests, hopes and dreams, and at least one prayer request for another person. Give them about ten minutes to do this, although I've seen groups get very engrossed and keep writing for much longer. Then give each an envelope with their name on, and seal the letter inside. Keep the letters – somewhere safe! Six months later, find a special, perhaps sacred time to open the letters together. Give each person ample time to read and digest their letter. As appropriate, either provide time for quiet prayer, or share anything interesting that reading the letters reveals.

Have prayers been answered? Have their relationships with God improved or worsened since the letters were written? If the activity goes really well, you may wish to close this time by writing a new set of letters, to be opened in another six months' time.

Week Two

Read: The Discipline of Study

2

"I have hidden your word in my heart that I might not sin against you."

Psalm 119:11

I'm not naïve. Of all the Disciplines, this may be the very toughest sell. On top of a life already jam-packed with homework, revision, and of course the relentlessness of school itself, is it really a good idea to suggest that "study" is something that young people need to practise more?

What if we frame things a different way, though? Because if study is something that young people are familiar with (I know, I didn't do nearly enough of it when I was at school either), then it is in fact the easiest Discipline to introduce, because it's a concept that young people already understand. More than that – teaching young people that study is a Spiritual Discipline can help them to see that spirituality and faith are not reserved for certain spaces, situations, and times of the week. The Discipline of Study helps teenagers to realize that school itself is spiritual – that God is at the very centre of their learning journey. Explained creatively and passionately, the Discipline of Study does not just equip young people with an extra incentive to work hard at school; far more importantly, it gives them a framework with which to wrestle with the Bible. With biblical literacy in rapid decline, it is perhaps vital that we rediscover ways of engaging young people enthusiastically with Scripture. Although it isn't the only application of this Discipline, it is perhaps the most pressing, and the best place to begin.

Struggling with the text

Do you ever find your eyes glazing over when you're trying to read something? Perhaps when you're tired at the end of a hard day, and you're trying desperately to read that "tremendously important" piece from the newspaper that a politically active friend has sent you? Or perhaps when you're halfway through what has turned out to be a very bad novel[5] and you can no longer be bothered to follow the story.

When I was a teenager, and a new Christian, I'm sad to say that this was often the effect that the Bible had on me. As a freshly reborn fourteen-year-old, I would sit in the study of my church's brilliant youth worker, and together we would look at sections from Mark's Gospel. He dedicated time to me every week, and I would try to understand the Bible better during that time.

Very little of that understanding, however, came from my own reading of the text. On his invitation, I would stare at the

---

5   See my 2004 allegorical football novel *England's Messiah* for a textbook example. Actually, you can't; they've wisely pulped it.

pages of my little red NIV, desperately trying to make sense of the words printed there. Yet there was only silence (not the deeply spiritual kind), and from then on it was a matter of waiting for his patience to finally give out, and some enlightening information to emerge from his lips.

Each week, he would explain the Bible to me. He did a great job of that, and particularly of putting up with me; each week he would start again by asking me what I thought the text was saying. Each week, however, I fear I rather disappointed him. I'm not sure what happened. Partly, I'm sure, that youth worker overestimated my intelligence, but also it was true that I never learned to value Bible study. Devotional or "quiet" times never quite made it into my busy adolescent schedule (for there was so much Super Nintendo to be played); I never did manage to "fall in love" with the Bible in the way that some of my friends seemed – or claimed – to have done.

One thing that I never quite grasped during my teens was the supernatural nature of the Bible. I had been taught to cherish it; in fact, perhaps some led me to worship it and make it a god in itself. This is of course a mistake – in one sense it's just a book, words on a printed page, one of many media. Many of us sometimes make that error of tripping across the fine line between loving the book and deifying it. As a teenager, this became something of a barrier to me – there was one way to read the book, one important meaning in each verse, and I wasn't quite getting them. I became intimidated, even guilty about the Bible.

I no longer believe that there is only one way to read the

Bible – that it has a single, surface layer of meaning which we either comprehend or misconstrue, obey or defy. The Rabbis call the Scriptures "the gem with a thousand faces" to illustrate the depth of meaning hidden within them, and Jesus Himself seems to suggest that the idea of studying and interpreting the Scriptures is perfectly natural:

"What is written in the Law?" he asks the expert in Luke 10:26; "How do you read it?"

What I never truly grasped was that the Bible is the living word of God. Not because the pages themselves are somehow inhabited by some supernatural force, but because, when we read them, God mysteriously meets with us by His Spirit, and speaks to us through the printed words. The recognition and practice of this is at the heart of the Discipline of Study. If we can help young people to read the Bible without burdening them with the misapprehension that there is only one "right" answer to be found in each passage, if we can liberate them in their reading of the Bible to realize that God Himself is their interpreter, and if we can give them time-honoured tools to help – perhaps it is not such an unrealistic hope that we might foster a love of the Bible in a generation that has supposedly rejected it.

Verbal and non-verbal

As I suggested at the beginning of this chapter, the study of the Scriptures is just one of the many applications of this Discipline. Like the Discipline of Meditation, with which it has a significant overlap, study is about approaching the world around us and "reading" it.

While mediation is concerned with contemplation, however, study is the practice of *analysis*. Through study we seek to read and comprehend – although "reading" may not simply refer to words on a page. The world of study is divided into two fields: verbal and non-verbal. The verbal side includes books, other media, and lectures; the non-verbal element (which is much larger) includes nature, art, and indeed other people. Richard Foster says that the task of study is to gain "a perception into the reality of a given situation, encounter, book, etc.". Through scrutiny and careful observation, we can learn so much – and this principle underpins the Discipline.

The four steps

In *Celebration of Discipline*, Foster outlines four steps that make up the Discipline of Study. These steps are applicable not only to the study of the Bible, but also to a range of verbal and non-verbal subjects.

The first step outlined by Foster is **Repetition**. This has a positive application to our reading of Scripture: the lost art of memory verses. For many, the memorizing of the Bible by recitation belongs in the realm of church holiday clubs; the Navigators' Topical Memory System no longer enjoys the popularity it had even twenty years ago. Yet Psalm 119:11 provides a picture of memorized Scripture ("I have hidden your word in my heart, Lord" says the psalmist) that we would do well to imitate, and the proven route to memorizing is through repetition.

In addition, scientific studies have proved that repetition of words and mantras – biblical and otherwise – leads to behaviour change in line with the statement repeated. In saying this I am not advocating indoctrination, of course; simply that, as we focus on and reassert the truth of Scripture, we are naturally and positively reaffirming its power in our lives.

The negative application of this step can be seen more passively, in the way that we consume media. If we expose ourselves to repeated images of violence, for instance, is it any wonder that we become more tense, perhaps more angry? I recently had to stop watching one of the many American "police procedural" TV series, because I realized that episode after episode of narratives and images based on murder and cruelty was having a disturbing effect on the way I viewed life. I began to become more afraid at night, double-checking the door and window locks each night because of an increased fear that my home might be invaded, and deliberately choosing to take a better-lit and more populated route home at night.

Why had I suddenly become such a bag of nerves? Because whatever we repeatedly put into our minds can have a profound effect on every part of us. Perhaps this is why the Bible says: "… whatever is pure, whatever is lovely, whatever is admirable… think about such things" (Philippians 4:8). To simplify, the first step of study is simply to bring our mind repeatedly to the subject matter in hand. If our mind wanders, if our thoughts stray, as they invariably do, we simply bring it back and focus once again. Through a commitment to doing so, we will inevitably learn something.

Of course, rote-learning is just the beginning. The second of Foster's steps is **Concentration**, by which we move from repeatedly returning to our subject to giving our full attention to it. To concentrate, which our minds are designed to do, is to behave counter-culturally, because we live in an age of distraction (see the next chapter for much more on this). We struggle to concentrate for long periods, and increasingly we struggle even to do one thing at a time. Even as I type these words, I am painfully aware that the BBC's *Newsnight* is blaring out in the background (OK, I've switched it off now). The younger generations in particular are very used to enjoying several stimuli at once – listening to their MP3 player while allegedly also being present at your Bible talk, for instance... However, if we are able to bring our minds to concentrate themselves, fully and at length, on one subject to the exclusion of others, then we open ourselves up to far greater learning and deeper understanding.

Foster's third step is **Comprehension**. In study, we seek not just to sustain our focus on a subject, but to understand it. Jesus Himself says in John 8:32 that it is the *knowledge* of the truth that sets us free, and comprehension is about gaining insight into the knowledge of the truth. Sometimes we are blessed with almost immediate understanding of a passage or subject; at other times it is through investing time and concentration that we finally move to a place of understanding.

Finally, we move towards **Reflection**. As Foster observes, while comprehension defines what we are studying, reflection determines the *significance* of what we are studying. This is where the Disciplines of Study and Meditation begin to merge, although here reflection is still part of a process of analysis, rather than contemplation. This final step in the activity of study is discerning the meaning of that which we are studying.

None of this exists in a vacuum. Like all the Disciplines, study still takes place within the context of an attitude of continual prayer. In each step, we consider and call on God to help us by His Spirit. It is He to whom we look for revelation at each step, and it is from Him that we gain the humility to remain teachable and open-minded as we practise the Discipline of Study through every stage of our lives.

Read: Resources

First steps – The discussion starter

NINETEEN DEGREES

Who is the most intelligent person in the world? It's a tough question to answer: some would suggest famous professors with great academic brains; others might opt for more emotionally intelligent individuals who can inspire many to follow them, such as Barack Obama or Nelson Mandela.

One Indian man, however, can at least claim to be the most educated person on earth. Ashoka Jahnavi Prasad is the proud owner of (at the time of counting) an incredible nineteen university qualifications, ranging from Master's degrees to doctorates. He has earned letters after his name from world-renowned institutions such as Oxford, Cambridge and St Andrews, and has served as a professor in New York, Zurich, Cambridge, and more. Even more incredibly, he had achieved all this by the age of fifty! An eminent scientist, Dr Prasad is a man of great personal discipline, a character trait which he has applied to both his study and his personal life. He is a strict vegetarian, and finds time to walk 10 kilometres every day. To have successfully completed this many academic courses, he is obviously also a big fan of revision.

Now in his fifties, Dr Prasad allegedly still lives with his mother. Considering that he spends so much time with his head in books, that hardly seems surprising. In truth, he has devoted the whole of his life to academic study – but does that mean he has lived life in all its fullness?

Opening up

Read the story above, then ask the following questions:

- Do you think Dr Prasad has made something great out of his life? Why?

- Do the sheer numbers of letters after his name make him a strong contender for the title of "most intelligent person in the world"?

- What might be some of the benefits of having so many qualifications?

- How do you feel about academic study? Is it enjoyable? Tiring? Something else?

- Do you ever study anything outside what you're asked to in school? Perhaps through a hobby or interest?

Digging deeper

- How do you feel about reading the Bible? How easy or difficult do you find it? Do you get much out of it?

- *How* do you read the Bible? Do you read it in sequence, or in random bits? Do you read things once, or several times over? What might be the effects of approaching Bible reading in these different ways?

Taking it to the word

Read Psalm 119:9–16

- What does it mean to hide God's word in your heart? How can you practically do that?

- What are some of the different ways in which these verses suggest we can engage with the Bible?

- How could we practically live out this passage in the way we handle the Bible? What new commitments could we make together?

The adaptable meeting guide

Meeting aim: To explore how study is not just an academic discipline but a varied spiritual one; to help young people to get their teeth into Bible reading with useable tools.

Before you start: You will need either a tray full of random objects or a ready-prepared PowerPoint™ presentation for the opening game; plenty of small chocolate prizes; Bibles for everyone; a card or piece of paper for every member of the group, with the word "concentrate" writ large across it; flip-chart paper and pen.

Game: What's missing?
(5 minutes)

You can run this activity in the old-school manner or give it a high-tech twist, depending on your style and budget. Get a tray of at least twelve to fifteen different objects, and give contestants one minute to memorize them. You then remove one object, and show them the tray again – can they spot which object is missing? Alternatively, create a PowerPoint™ presentation of ten or so random famous people / film stills / album covers, etc., and play it through to the group. Now play it again, this time removing one of the images – can they work out which one is missing? This game provides a gentle way in to a session looking at our ability to study, concentrate, and comprehend.

What can you study?
(5 minutes)

Ask the group: what do they think of when they hear the word "study"? School work? Exam revision? Now ask: what else can you study besides textbooks and school subjects? What does it mean to study nature, for instance – or people? Explain that study is a discipline, and that while it is one of the hardest, it is not just an academic discipline, but also a spiritual one. God has given us a complicated world to live in, and a living Word to engage with and understand. Neither are simple or straightforward; both reward an investment of study.

A four-step Bible study (25 minutes total)

Explain that in this session we are going to look at one of the most famous passages in the New Testament, and part of the most remarkable sermon ever preached: Jesus' Sermon on the Mount. This section, Matthew 5:1–12, is known as "the Beatitudes" (the word "beatitude" literally means "blessedness"). Many people have commented that this strange old word breaks down nicely into "Be Attitudes" – and this is a great way to sum the passage up, because Jesus is telling the people how they should "be". In this activity, we will be using a tried-and-tested method for studying the Bible. We all struggle sometimes to understand what the Bible is saying and how it applies to us; here are four complementary approaches to getting better connected with the word of God.

Step one: Repetition

The first step is about learning by repetition. Years ago this used to be one of the major activities of Christian youth groups – and we shouldn't have left it behind. Learning by rote helps us to "hide God's word in our hearts" (Psalm 119:11). Read the passage through. Now ask each group to pick a section containing as many verses as there are group members. Give them five minutes to memorize the passage through repetition together. Either they can take one verse each, or – if they want to go for a bigger prize – they can attempt to memorize the entire section together. Get the groups to "perform" their verses, and hand out small chocolate prizes for those who manage a verse, and larger prizes (you probably won't need many of these!) for any group that manages the entire passage.

Step two: Concentration

Give each young person a Bible, and a card with the word "concentrate" written on it. Ask them to find a quiet space somewhere in the building, and set them the challenge of reading the passage over and over again for the next five minutes. Set tight rules for this: they must not talk; they must not look at their phone; they must only read the passage specified: Matthew 5:1–11. If they start to feel distracted, they should look at the card, say the word "concentrate" under their breath, and then return to the passage. They should be able to get through it several times in the five minutes.

Step three: Comprehension

They will now have read or heard the passage between five and ten times. In groups, ask them to analyse the story together, by asking some key questions. They should answer not simply with direct quotes from the Scripture, but in their own words.

- What are Jesus' main points in this part of His sermon?

- What detail can we pick up? Who is He talking to? Where are they geographically?

• What do you think is the theme of this passage?

Give them about five minutes for this part of the discussion, then move on to the reflection activity.

Step four: Reflection

Ask them to remain in their groups for a second discussion, but this time, instead of looking at the who, what and why of the passage, we're going to reflect on what it means to us, now. Everyone in the room will now have read the passage many times. Now, since they have become so familiar with the words, ask them to close their Bibles. Ask everyone to spend two minutes in silence, thinking about the meaning of the passage they've been reading. In the quiet, they might want to ask God to reveal something new to them. After the short silence, ask them to discuss some final questions:

• What does this passage mean for followers of Jesus today?

• What especially struck you out of everything you read?

• What do you think God might be saying to you through these verses?

These are much deeper questions, and they may warrant further reflection. Invite your group to consider reflecting on them over the coming week, and offer to pick up the thread again at the beginning of the next session.

As you finish this section, make sure that everyone has understood that this four-step approach to Bible study is now something they can use each time they open the Bible in their own time. Invite them to try it for themselves with another passage over the coming week.

Beyond the Bible (10 minutes)

Explain that the Discipline of Study isn't just limited to our analysis of the Bible, although that is perhaps the first and most important thing we can study. We can use this Spiritual Discipline to better understand two huge "worlds". The first is the written, academic world, which includes school subjects; the second is the natural, non-verbal world – in which for instance we can study nature and other people. On flip-chart paper at the front, create a simple grid, with the four steps along one axis, and four examples of fields of study on the others. So the first axis should read: Repetition, Concentration, Comprehension, Reflection; the second axis could read: Tree, History Book, Friend, Poem. Say that study helps us not only to understand the world around us, but to see God in every part of it. How might you practically use the Discipline to study each of these things?

Taking suggestions from the floor, fill in the grid.

What does this mean for me? (5 minutes)

As you finish the session, ask each person to share with their neighbour which of the four steps has most caught their imagination, and how they can see themselves making use of it in the future. Pray to close, asking God to give all of you more discipline when it comes to reading, learning and absorbing, with regard to both the Bible and the world that He has given us.

ADAPTING THE MATERIAL

For older groups... You might hold a longer discussion about where God fits into our school studies. Can you find God in maths for instance, or physics? How could the Discipline of Study help with this?

For younger groups... There is a lot of discussion and reading, so you may want to focus the session solely on the Bible (don't cut out any of the four steps). Alternatively, throw in an energizing game in the middle; perhaps a concentration game such as "wink murder".

For churchgoing young people... Challenge the group to put the four steps into practice in the week ahead, but not with their interaction with the Bible. Instead, ask them to use it as a method of academic study, or of looking again at some part of nature that they have previously taken for granted.

For unchurched young people... Hold the session outdoors, and spend more time looking at nature. Have the group run through the four steps with a leaf, stream or tree, then explain how this can also be used as a system to help make sense of the Bible.

Going deeper: Follow-on activities

1. MEMORY CHALLENGE

Reinstate the classic principle of memory verses with your youth group! At the start of a new term, create a sheet split into twelve squares – printed on card if you can. In each box, write out a key Bible verse which you would like your group to memorize. You could take as themes for these the promises of God, or verses about wisdom, or anything you think your group particularly needs to remember. When you meet, hold a short discussion about the verses: which do they like best? Which do they think would be most or least memorable? Make sure they understand what the verses are saying. While you're still together, cut the sheets up so that everyone is left with a set of twelve cards. Challenge them over the next three months to see if they can memorize one verse a week through repetition – encourage them to spur each other on and test one another. At the end of the term, offer a decent prize to anyone who can recite all twelve verses back to you.

2. SPIRITUAL REVISION

In the lead-up to exams, hold a revision night which makes use of the fourth step of the Discipline of Study: reflection. Invite your young people to bring their textbooks along to your meeting, and begin with a prayer, asking God to reveal Himself through the things the young people are studying and revising. Spend half an hour under exam conditions, with leaders acting as "invigilators". During that time, ask your group to read and revise with an awareness that God is at the heart of every academic subject. He created it, He operates through it, and it is entirely His. If "the earth is the Lord's, and everything in it" (Psalm 24:1), what does that mean for the subject that you're revising tonight? After the half-hour is up, gather together for a drink (and maybe some doughnuts if you're feeling generous) and ask:

- What did you learn about your subject?

- What did you learn about God?

If time allows, repeat the activity for another thirty minutes. While this shouldn't be the only way young people prepare for their exams, it is a great way of practically demonstrating that God is not separate from their school subjects – He's right there at the heart of them.

Week Three

Listen: The Discipline of Meditation

"Be still, and know
that I am God;
I will be exalted among the
nations,
I will be exalted in the
*   earth."*

Psalm 46:10

As we begin to look at the Disciplines over a period of time, we cannot fail to be struck by how counter-cultural they are: fasting in a world obsessed with consumption; simplicity in a world that celebrates its own ever-increasing complexity. In the case of the Discipline of Meditation, however, we can find more cultural touchstones. Popular psychology positively recommends meditation as a practice of gazing into one's own soul in search of meaning. Self-help and New Age enthusiasts might mix it with chanting, astrology, hypnotism and a range of other additives.

The Christian Discipline of Meditation, however, is much more simple. It is, in the most straightforward terms, the practice of listening to and thinking about God. Quite often, although not exclusively, it becomes the practice of reflecting on His word – although not interrogating the text as we might through the Discipline of Study. It is about taking time out to reflect, pray, notice and hear. It is about quieting our own voice, and listening out for the still small voice of our creator. To dedicate time to meditation is to dedicate time to a friendship with Jesus, just as we might devote quality time to a close friend or family member in order to get to know them better. As we meditate on what we know, what we are learning, and what others have said about God, we cannot fail to be drawn more closely toward Him. The Bible mentions meditation repeatedly as a natural pursuit of the faithful. Isaac goes out into the field to meditate in Genesis 24:63; the psalmists often turn to the word to describe how God's people dedicate themselves to thinking about God and His Law. Meditation might have been adopted and adapted by modern "spirituality", but its practice is profoundly biblical.

Meditation is perhaps the simplest Discipline – it is really just about thinking and listening in an attitude of quiet reflection. Yet because the person you are thinking about and listening to is God Himself, it is also possibly the richest and most profound experience you can have. To meditate is to invest in our inner life; like the Discipline of Study, it concerns us with focusing and concentrating our minds on one thing, a practice that may not come naturally to many of us.

I have developed a modern condition which my friend Sarah Wynter calls "Open Windows Syndrome". It expresses itself in the way I use a computer, because I'll often have countless windows (yes, I'm a PC; I can't afford a Mac) open at the same time. My mind gets distracted easily; it flits between focuses like a fourteen-year-old who's had one too many energy drinks. At the end of a working day, I often find that I have started several different emails without ever getting round to finishing or sending any of them. I have four different documents open; my web browser is packed with tabs from the websites I've visited but haven't bothered to leave. In short, my end-of-day desktop reflects the fractured nature of my attention span – all day long I've tried to do everything at once, and as a result I have failed to be half as dynamic as I could have been. It's not just my computer, though, that bears witness to my fleeting mind. If I'm not careful, my relationships can too. "Open Windows Syndrome" isn't just about how I work – it's also the way that I too often approach conversations with my friends and family. Because of the pace of our lives, because of the speed at which we're used to receiving information and media (and even food!), we do not need to develop self-discipline in the area of concentration. So, as I talk, my words can sometimes lack direction; as I listen, I am easily distracted by a stray thought that has just popped back into my head. Sometimes I keep as many windows open in my head as I do on my desktop.

The Discipline of Meditation addresses this modern problem head-on.

It requires us to look at things and really see them, to focus on a single idea way beyond the limits of our usual attention span. It is the process of rediscovering a muscle that either has never been developed or went flabby a long time ago; it is the act of cultivating concentration. Some of us, especially extroverts like myself, can find the idea of stopping to think and wonder extremely threatening. Yet in a world that moves so fast, the

Discipline of Meditation can be liberating. Taking our time over our thoughts, our reflections, our prayers, is a profound skill that has become somewhat lost to the world. Meditation reawakens it.

Choosing focus

Meditation can generally focus us in one of three directions; towards God, towards our inner selves, or towards Scripture.

Meditating on God involves slowing ourselves right down and reflecting solely on His character. We remember His promises to us; we bring to mind the things that we know about Him. The cross of Christ is perhaps the most natural focus for our meditation; the sacrifice of God's only Son is a fitting subject for reverent, silent thought and prayer. Equally we can bring to mind the reality of His resurrection, and all that this means for us as His followers.

Inward reflection gives us space to put our own lives under the microscope. This is not introspective self-obsession; it is a chance to look at how God lives within us; to see where He has already affected and changed us, and where He is still at work, refining our characters. This inward meditation is a kind of spiritual health check, which we can sometimes neglect to perform on ourselves, but if we are to claim that God has changed and is changing us, perhaps it is helpful to truly understand for ourselves how. Inward meditation is the process of reflecting on our own ongoing transformation through the power of God.

Meditating on Scripture is different from the Discipline of Studying the Bible. This is not the act of rigorously interrogating the text, but rather the practice of allowing God to speak to us through His word. Scriptural meditation taps in to the living quality of the word of God – the fact that the Spirit interprets and clarifies the enduring message of the Bible to us. A word of warning, though – scriptural meditation should not be performed in isolation. Rather, we should bring to it an attitude of continuous prayer, and a commitment to reading and understanding passages in context. The alternative is that we choose a few words, phrases, or verses and, without seeking to know their context, expect them to enlighten us. This is a dangerous practice, and can lead us to a place of misunderstanding, rather than enlightenment.

Still, the Disciplines offer us two complementary routes to approaching the Bible, and we should ignore neither – we should both seek to better understand the Scriptures, and allow them to speak to us as the divine word of God.

Getting started

Perhaps the idea of meditation is new to you. If so, it would be a good idea to practise the Discipline yourself before teaching it to others. What follows is a very simple meditation exercise, which requires no resources apart from a comfortable place to sit.

In a moment, put this book down and find yourself a quiet place, preferably one in which you won't be disturbed for at least twenty minutes. Find a comfortable chair, or a spot on the floor, and get into a position that you'll be happy to hold for a long time without becoming distracted. Place your hands, palms down, on your knees or in your lap. Remove anything from the room that might steal your attention, such as a mobile phone or wristwatch. Close your eyes, and focus on your breathing as you allow your body to relax. Breathe slowly and deeply, and allow your body to move into a state of rest.

Now, in an attitude of prayer, begin to bring to mind the time in your life when you made a conscious decision to follow Christ. Perhaps a specific day doesn't spring immediately to mind, but a time in your life does. Focus on that period: who you were; the person you had been before you found faith; the immediate changes that took place in you around that time. In the silence, take your mind on a journey from that point, through the spiritual milestones in your life: the important relationships; the church communities you've been a part of; the stories of answered prayer; the hard times when God seemed far away. As slowly, and in as much detail, as you can manage, retell to yourself the story of your Christian faith. Allow yourself to dwell on memories that you had half-forgotten, and enjoy tracing the pattern of God's involvement in your life. At the end of this time, thank God for the things that you have remembered; and perhaps make a note of anything that has struck you.

Meditation doesn't even need to be as complicated as the exercise above. It could mean no more than spending an extra ten minutes at the end of a daily Bible reading, simply rereading the text and asking God to speak through it. The important thing is that we begin to take on an attitude of prayerful reflection, slowing ourselves down to the point that we can begin to hear that "gentle whisper" (1 Kings 19:12) that is God speaking to us.

Listen: Resources

First steps – The discussion starter

MEDITATION MAN

David Lynch is one of the world's most acclaimed film-makers and TV directors, having created a huge range of cult classics from *The Elephant Man* to *Twin Peaks*. He has been at the top of his game for well over thirty years, winning legions of fans – and for many in the entertainment world he is held up as a great inspiration and role model. So how has he managed it? How has he enjoyed so many critical hits, and seen his name become synonymous with cool, quirky film-making? In his opinion at least, the secret lies in his long-held passion for meditation. Since 1975, Lynch has been an advocate of "transcendental" meditation – a form of quiet reflection that involves the repetition of certain "mantras" or sounds in order to enlighten the mind – believing that it is the key to bringing order and peace to the world. He himself practises meditation daily, spending fifteen to twenty minutes each morning and evening reciting the mantras, and he believes this to be the source of his continued creativity.

Lynch dedicates much of his time to convincing others of the need to join him in this practice. This is where it gets a little… strange, though, for, like many devotees of transcendental meditation, he believes that the power of positive peaceful meditative thought is somehow able to bring peace to the world. He doesn't believe that this is because those thoughts are connecting with God – but that somehow the positive energy of the meditations themselves can be a force for change. So convinced is Lynch that meditation is the missing element of modern life that he's even set up a Foundation to help young people in America to learn the technique for themselves. As he explains on the Foundation's website,[6] meditation is the one activity that opens up "the full brain"; he believes that, in doing so, we can at the same time change ourselves and change the world.

Opening up

Read the story above, and then ask the following questions:

- What do you make of David Lynch's theory that meditation could change the world?

- How might clearing your mind and repeating "mantras" open up "the full brain"?

- Why do you think Lynch is so keen to convince others of the power of meditation?

Digging deeper

- Have you ever meditated? What did you do, and what happened?

- What is meditation? How could it practically become a part of your day/life? Do you think you could give up fifteen minutes, twice a day to it? What might happen if you did?

---

6 http://www.davidlynchfoundation.org/

Taking it to the word

Read Psalm 46

- Look particularly at verse 10. What does it mean to become still in order to truly "know" something?

- How does this verse help to connect David Lynch's theory about meditation with a relationship with God? What might "Christian meditation" look like, and how is it different from what Lynch is proposing?

- If you wanted to try meditation out, this psalm could provide a great entry point. Take yourself off into a comfortable, quiet place with no distractions. Read the psalm slowly, three or four times. Allow the words to wash over you, to speak to you. Afterwards, debrief together: how was that experience for you? What happened?

The adaptable meeting guide

Meeting aim: To explore what Christian meditation is; to explode the myth that it's far too slow, silent and boring to work for young people; to spend some time practising the Discipline of Meditation.

Before you start: You will need paints, A3 paper, and any other material you can find to put on a really enjoyable art activity – equip yourself as if you were running a Messy Church session, or teaching a primary school art lesson! You will also need pens and paper, and enough Bibles for everyone.

Create!
(20 minutes)

Explain that, at the start of this meeting, we're going to have a chance to unleash our inner child, and enjoy a primary-school-style art session. Equip your meeting venue with as much paint, glue, collage materials, sponges, potatoes (for potato printing) etc. as you can manage. Have all this set out so that when your group arrives they are immediately excited and can start getting their hands dirty. Give them all at least fifteen minutes to create a work of poster-sized art, using any of the materials provided. The only stipulation is that the artwork must be inspired by the Bible verse: **"I tell you the truth, he who believes has everlasting life"** – John 6:47 (have this verse written on a large piece of paper in a visible position). When the time is up, put the artwork somewhere to dry, and instigate a big clean-up. Don't leave this until afterwards – they will be happy to clean up their mess, and it will save you being at the venue until midnight.

What is meditation?
(5 minutes)

Bring the group together again, and ask them what they understand by the word "meditation". Perhaps they are aware of the Transcendental Meditation movement (you might want to refer to the Discussion Starter earlier in this chapter), or know that meditation is practised by many people interested in a wide variety of spiritual traditions and practices. In its broadest sense, it is about quieting ourselves and connecting with internal and external forces to help us think and reflect. Explain that in this, very practical, session, they're going to have a chance to try three "directions" of Christian meditation. In simple terms, the Christian Discipline of Meditation is concerned with thinking about and listening to God in an attitude of quiet reflection. The next three activities will help us to do that together.

Meditating on God
(10 minutes)

In the first activity, we are going to take everything that we know already about God – His character and what He has done – and spend a few minutes thinking about these things. This might include what we know from reading the Bible, from seeing Him work in the lives of other people, from looking at creation, and from remembering stories that we've been told. To give the young people a focus, ask them to spend just a minute writing down their responses to the question: what is God like? No one else will see their answers – this is purely between them and God. As much as is possible, invite your young people to spread out around your venue or building.

Once they have written their responses, invite them to make themselves comfortable, in a space where they are separate from other members of the group. Suggest that they switch off (or even hand over) mobile phones and other devices, and remove other distractions where possible. Now invite them to spend a few minutes thinking about the things that they have written on their piece of paper. They shouldn't simply stare at their answers, but allow their thoughts to go off in whatever direction they want to. The aim is to listen, through these thoughts, to what God might be saying. After five minutes, stop the exercise and ask the young people to make any further notes on their paper of things that struck them or seemed important while they were reflecting on God's character in this way.

Inward reflection (15 minutes)

For the second activity, ask the group to pair up – each person preferably joining with someone who doesn't know the ins and outs of their partner's life story. After a few moments' thinking time, the first person in each pair should talk for one minute about their "journey of faith", up to and including any clear moment of "decision", taking in the lows and moments of doubt, remembering the times when God has stepped in and/or answered prayers. However, point out that this is not, as it might appear, a listening activity – it is designed instead to help us to remember our own stories through telling them. After a minute, allow a few moments for the listener to ask any questions they may have. Then ask the pairs to swap roles, so that the listener becomes the speaker.

After everyone has told their story to someone, ask them to return to the meditation position that they adopted in the previous exercise. Again, they have five minutes to think and reflect; this time they are meditating on the story that they have *told* – not the one they have heard. If they need more help, suggest that they picture themselves as a new Christian, then begin to visualize the different stages and landmark moments of their lives since, and where God has been involved. How has God changed them? At the end of five minutes, invite them to return to their pair briefly, and share any extra details of their stories that struck them while they were meditating.

Meditating on Scripture (10 minutes)

Give out Bibles, and ask them to read Mark 4:35–41 (Jesus calms the storm). Explain that, when they return to their quiet space, they should first relax, and then read the text through very slowly. Then they should read the text a second time, and as their eyes wander over the page they should allow themselves to notice any word or phrase that seems to stand out to them. They should then focus on that phrase, and reflect on it in prayer – asking God what He might be saying through it.

Reflection into action (5 minutes)

Bring the group back together, and remind everyone of the three meditations. Ask those who are comfortable with sharing: what were some of the things that God seemed to be saying during these times of reflection? Issue the group a challenge: what are you going to *do* as a result of what God has said to you through this session? What practical steps might you take in response? As you close, give out the (hopefully now dry) works of art which you made together at the start of the session. Explain that these are intended to be a resource for them as they look to experiment with meditation in the weeks ahead. These pictures can be a helpful focal point for their meditations: encourage them to take the picture to a quiet place at some point in the week ahead, and spend at least fifteen minutes – more if they can – reflecting on why they created this picture in this way, and what God might now be saying back to them through it.

ADAPTING THE MATERIAL

For older groups... It might seem counter-intuitive to ask young people to be silent for extended periods, but I have tried these exercises and they work. Young people live up to our expectations of them – so make those expectations high! With older groups, consider extending the meditation activities to fifteen or even twenty minutes – even if that means doing only two of the three.

For younger groups... In the "meditating on Scripture" activity, have the group together, rather than separated into their quiet spaces. Get them quiet and relaxed, and then explain that, as you read the passage from Mark, you want them to imagine themselves in the story. Encourage them to really get into it – what can they see? What does the place smell, sound, and feel like? Read the story slowly and dramatically, pausing at any moments of description or drama. Leave a pause, and then ask the young people what struck them during the reading.

For churchgoing young people... At the end of the session, encourage the young people to build the Discipline of Meditation into the week ahead. Apart from looking at their artwork, can they find thirty minutes to repeat the activities you've run in this session? Have a catch-up at the beginning of the following session, to see what happened.

For unchurched young people… This session might be a real stretch for those who aren't already Christians. Run the discussion session from the First Steps section of this chapter instead, or strip the session down so that it simply includes the first activity, the explanation of what meditation is, and then a short time of quiet, reflecting on their works of art and why they painted/created them in this way.

Going deeper: Follow-on activities

1. FACES OF CHRIST

This simple activity could work with non-Christian young people as well as with those who already have a faith. Using the power of an Internet image search, find a number of good-quality images of Jesus. You may want to use only paintings, or you could include film stills from the various big-screen productions about Jesus' life. Print these out so that each image doesn't quite fill an A4 sheet, but has a wide margin around the edge. Make sure that you have enough sheets for everyone to have one. Lay all the images out on the table, and first invite your group to look through the various interpretations and images of Jesus that art and film have produced. Now ask everyone to pick one of the images, and take it into a quiet space. They should spend three to five minutes looking at the image, noticing every detail, and allowing God to speak to them through it. Then, after the set time has elapsed, they can annotate the margins of the sheet with everything that strikes them as interesting or profound about the image, or anything they feel they might have heard God say. Alternatively, if you don't have time to go trawling for images, find the 1851 portrait of Jesus by the Belgian artist Albert Roberti, or another picture of your choice, and make copies for everyone.

2. PALMS DOWN, PALMS UP

In his amazing book *Celebration of Discipline*, Richard Foster outlines a simple meditation activity that can help to form an attitude of reflective prayer. Explain to your group that this is a physical prayer involving only your hands, which means you can do it practically any time, anywhere – even in a public place if you're feeling brave! We all walk around weighed down by the pressures of stuff we're worried about. So those things provide the most natural springboard for asking for God's help.

This activity will help you to identify the things you're concerned about, and the ways in which you know deep down that God can help you. Either prepare a simple sheet with the two boxes below, or ask the group to create it for themselves. In this first box, ask them to write all the things they can think of that are getting them down, stressing them out, or causing them to fear or worry. Examples: relationship issues, school or college problems, work pressures, etc.

God, I release to You:

Now, in the second box, ask them to remember and write down the gifts and good things that God has promised to give us when we ask. Examples: His love, His peace, wisdom, the Holy Spirit.

God, I receive from You:

Now, as they sit with these two lists in front of them, ask them to hold their hands out, with their palms facing the floor. Read out: "God, I release to You" – and leave a pause, during which they can look over their first list and release these things to God. Emphasize to them the power of releasing all these concerns to Him. He's a lot bigger than all this stuff, and He can handle it! Ask the group to turn their palms up the other way, and read the second statement. This time, keep them in this position for as long as feels comfortable. Encourage them to receive from God all the things that He has promised to give to them.

This simple exercise helps us to remember two important truths – that God wants us to cast our burdens onto Him (1 Peter 5:7), and that He longs to give us good gifts that will sustain and help us (Matthew 7:7–11). It also allows us not only to learn about the value of prayer, but to step in and begin engaging in its power. We learn through doing that there is great value in involving God – even if only very briefly – in the details of our lives.

Week Four

Refrain: The Discipline of Fasting

"When you fast, do not look sombre as the hypocrites do, for they disfigure their faces to show others they are fasting. Truly I tell you, they have received their reward in full. But when you fast, put oil on your head and wash your face, so that it will not be obvious to others that you are fasting, but only to your Father, who is unseen; and your Father, who sees what is done in secret, will reward you."

Matthew 6:16–18 (TNIV)

We live in an age of consumption and consumerism. Technology manufacturers focus clever advertising campaigns on getting you to buy their latest gadget, only to tell you eighteen months later that the same item is redundant, and has been superseded by one even greater. Fast-food retailers offer the option of "going large" as standard, even when a regular-sized meal would have been quite enough. Children are marketed to from the moment they can talk, and as a result many of them begin their vocabulary with the words "I want". Actually, "iWant" would be a good name for a gadget, because so much of the technology market is about selling us things we want, rather than need (more on this when we look at the Discipline of Simplicity).

For (controversial) instance: no one, in my opinion, truly *needs* an iPad (the irony that you might be reading this on one is not lost on me). They are beautiful pieces of gadgetry; they do lots of things that make us gasp and smile, and I really, really want one. But an iPad doesn't actually do anything that you can't do already. It has some of the functions of a laptop, which are available at around a third of the price; it allows us to read books and magazines on the go, which, of course, is exactly the functionality of books and magazines. It doesn't really *do* anything. But it's beautiful, and desperately clever, and so many of us would love to own one.

My point isn't, however, that the iPad exists. It's that just a few short months after the machine was released, it was upgraded. iPad 2 appeared, offering slightly better features (such as a built-in camera), and gently taunted owners of the now-inferior original model. Are you really satisfied with version one, it asked them slyly? Immediately, many of the device's owners could not stand the sense of being behind the times, listed their "old" iPads on eBay and jumped aboard the version-two bandwagon. When version three inevitably appears (I dread to think how things might have evolved by the time you read this), they may be unable to resist doing the same again.

In his book *Generation X*,[7] novelist Douglas Coupland refers to the homewares sold by one well-known megastore as "semi-disposable Swedish furniture". In a society that has to keep selling us stuff in order to keep its financial model working, companies are incentivized to place a virtual or literal "expiry date" on any and every item we buy. This disposable culture drives an inevitable attitude of consumption. This is what twenty-first-century humans do: we consume. We don't stop there, though. We don't just consume; we consume *gluttonously*. We buy, horde, and eat far more than we need. I spent a great deal of my student loans on obscure CDs I no longer listen to and VHS cassettes that I couldn't now watch even if I wanted to. I am a recovering Collector of Things; I dread to think how much money I wasted in my youth on video games, comics and Dr Who memorabilia. The continuing success of capitalism seems to suggest it's not just me: we are set up in Western society to purchase far more than we will ever need. The industries of advertising, retail, technology, banking and a hundred more demand that we consume gluttonously.

And all this takes place in the context of a culture of entitlement. We in the West are subtly fed the idea that our human rights extend far beyond those protected by the Geneva

---

7   Published by St Martin's Griffin, 1991.

Convention or any national constitution. We don't just have a right to freedom of thought, speech and expression; we believe we have a right to cheap fuel, to employment and prosperity, to do whatever it is that we want to do. Just as consumption and gluttony focus not on what we need but on what we want, entitlement means that we are never satisfied solely with what is good and right for us. We want more, and if we want it, we should be allowed to have it.

The Discipline of Fasting stands opposed to our culture of consumption, gluttony and entitlement. Primarily focused on our relationship with food, this Discipline can be widened to address the problems we might have with the consumption of a great number of things, from having a bulging shoe collection to downloading an unfeasibly large collection of iPhone apps.

It is perhaps no surprise that there is little place for the idea of fasting – of willingly going without – in the modern world. Yet it was a common practice at the time of Jesus, and up to the last 200 years or so it was an established part of the Christian life. The fact that this now-neglected aspect of faith is so frequently mentioned in the Bible should give us a huge clue that it needs to be readdressed.

Fasting is modelled by Jesus who, in Luke 4, spends forty days without food ("he ate nothing" – verse 2) but not water (the same verse tells us that he was "hungry" but not thirsty). Physically, then, total abstention from food for a period – from one mealtime upwards – is the biblical picture. There are a few examples of absolute fasts in the Bible, where both food and water are abstained from, but these are very specific circumstances (such as Esther 4:16), and constitute the exception rather than the rule in the context of many other mentions of fasting. In most cases of fasting, the individuals and peoples involved are choosing to sacrifice their regular intake of food in order to become closer to God, to demonstrate their commitment to Him and to focus their bodies and minds on heaven.

Why fast?

We will look briefly at two approaches to fasting: the self-denial of food, which is matched by the biblical description of "fast"; and then the limitation or removal from our lives of those things that might get in the way of our relationship with God. This latter form of fasting is popularly practised by Christians of various denominations during the Lent period. First, though, we should ask the question: why fast? How does this process of self-denial bring us closer to God?

The first answer of course is the biblical mandate, which some would argue could even be read as a command. In Matthew 6:16, Jesus refers to "when you fast", which seems to make the assumption that all followers of God should build the practice into their "devotional" life. Secondly, though, we have the experience of centuries of believers to draw on – men and women who saw fasting as central to the process of spiritual formation, who practised it regularly, and who saw and recorded the fruit of doing so. Fasting draws us closer to God because it both demonstrates our commitment to taking Him seriously and gives us a tangible reminder that we are devoted, and a method through which we can focus. Our physical hunger draws us toward prayer; the rattling emptiness of our usually-full stomachs gives us a sense of spirituality, and, although that might sound rather daft, it is not to be ignored. God works in those feelings of hunger; He meets us even in a place of small sacrifice.

Fasting also purifies us. It takes away something that we can live without for a while, and invites us to focus energies that might usually be concerned with consumption upon the One who sustains our every breath. The ultimate answer to the question of what it is that I truly need, rather than want, is a living relationship with God. Everything else will fall away. Whether we are fasting from food or television, the choice to prioritize what our spirit needs over what our body wants is a profound one.

Food

The most obvious form of gluttony is seen in our relationship with food, whether that be binge-eating or too-great a passion for cheese. The philosopher Socrates said that "Bad men live that they may eat and drink, whereas good men eat and drink that they may live".[8] Driven by the consumption culture, we can develop unhealthy attitudes to food that can lead to both physical and emotional problems, including, of course, eating disorders and obesity. Yet fasting recognizes that this is also a spiritual issue, and is a tool that can help us to restore balance to the way we treat food. A word of warning though – food is a major issue for a number of young people, and we need to exercise extreme care when talking about it. Fasting could easily be used as a way for a young (or older) person to legitimize an eating disorder in their

---

8   From Plutarch, *How a Young Man Ought to Hear Poems*.

own mind by spiritualizing it, and this needs to be taken into account when we encourage young people to become involved in this Discipline.

For this reason, I would strongly recommend that as we teach the practice of fasting to young people, we explore it in short measures. Young people can be asked to fast for a meal, and perhaps (as with World Vision's 24-hour Famine events) a whole day, ending of course with a hearty breakfast. But I would advise against exploring longer fasts with young people. Because in most cases they are still growing, their bodies will suffer from food withdrawal more quickly than adults' will. For various reasons, while it is good to teach the principle of food-fasting to young people, we should keep the practice of it relatively brief. In small doses, however, the Discipline of Fasting is a great way for young people to enjoy a more experiential prayer time, to show God and themselves how important their faith is, and to check whether their own relationship with food has become warped.

Beyond food

We can also explore with young people other areas of consumption. In each case we ask the question: how can what we watch, play, buy and do get in the way of our relationship with God? Sometimes the answer is that one takes priority over the other; at other times our consumption of things can distract and even lead us in the opposite direction to God. A video-game "addiction", for instance, can lead a young person to fill their time with violent, sexualized, and far-from-edifying game play. Fasting can help us to practically address a discipleship issue like this, as we take a break from a behaviour that is perhaps drawing a young person away from God, and replace it with a commitment to spending time with Him. Lent, for instance, is not just about giving something up for forty days, but also about taking something "holy" up in its place. Fasting creates a vacuum in the life of a young person, into which God can move.

Refrain: Resources

First steps – The discussion starter

FAST FOOD

Chad Bulger has a special gift. He is not the world's brightest man; he confesses he has always been terrible at sport; he is terrified of public speaking. Yet there is one thing that Chad can do more, better and faster than almost anyone: eat.

Twenty-five-stone Chad hails from the American Mid-West, where he was raised by his mother, a waitress in a small-town diner. Chad's mum had it tough: she had to raise him alone while working long, punishing shifts at the restaurant. By necessity, Chad would eat most of his meals there, and as a result of his daily bowlfuls of fried stuff (with a side order of molten cheese), he began to grow in more ways than just vertically.

That didn't bother Chad, though – he developed a love for food, and, like so many of us, much preferred the less nutritious options. Mrs Bulger realized after a while that she was endangering her son's health through his diet, but the damage was already done. Chad was now hooked on food, and on eating as much of it as possible.

Chad didn't realize that he was "gifted", however, until he was introduced to the glamorous world of competitive eating. After winning a high-school pie-devouring contest by an alarming margin, he was taken under the wing of a retired local champion, who coached him towards greater glory. Soon afterwards, Chad began competing in International Federation of Competitive Eating (IFOCE) events around the USA, a pursuit which now dominates his year, as well as that of his proud mum.

Chad says his dream now is to win possession of the coveted "Mustard Belt" – the Wimbledon trophy of the competitive eating world. At present he is not considered one of the greats of the "sport", but he hopes that, with training, he might one day rank alongside his heroes – men like California's Joey Chestnut and "the Notorious B.O.B.", Bob Shoudt of Philadelphia.

"I'm only twenty-four," Chad told reporters, "so I've got time on my side." Let's hope he's right.

Opening up

Read the story above, and then ask the following questions:

- How do you feel about Chad after hearing that story?

- Is there a sense in which he has made something amazing of his life?

- Apart from the obvious health reasons, why might eating as much as Chad does be bad for a person?

Digging deeper

- What is your attitude to food? Do you live to eat, or eat to live?

- What do you know about fasting? Have you ever tried it?

- What are some of the reasons why occasional fasting might be a good idea?

- What are some of the other things, apart from food, that a person might fast or abstain from (think about what people might give up at Lent)?

- What might be some examples of gluttony (excessive consumption) in modern culture that don't involve food?

Taking it to the word

Read Luke 4:1–8

- Why do you think Jesus chose to fast for forty days? What did this achieve?

- What is the connection between the first temptation and the second? Where is Jesus putting His trust?

- How does fasting help Him here – and us today – to get our priorities right?

- Find an opportunity to miss one meal (making sure you eat two other large, nutritious meals that day), and instead use the time to pray and focus on God. What do you experience as a result?

The adaptable meeting guide

Meeting aim: To explore the biblical concept of fasting; to understand how it applies today both with regard to food and in other applications.

Before you start: This subject must be treated carefully, as young people do not always have a healthy relationship with food. Make sure you are aware of any special dietary considerations, and any problems some of them may have with either over- or under-eating. For the session you will need plenty of magazines, catalogues and takeaway menus featuring pictures of gadgets, hip clothes, fast food, lots of things manufactured by Apple, and other "must-have" items; glue, scissors and paper; foods of your choice for "extreme chubby bunnies"; and a good, honest guest for the "power of hunger" section.

Extreme chubby bunnies (5 minutes)

Everyone loves the classic youth-work staple in which two contestants try to cram more marshmallows into their mouth than the other person, while still being able to say "chubby bunnies". It remains a great way of illustrating the dangers of gluttony – that overstuffing ourselves with food can inhibit our ability to behave normally. We're going to spice things up, however, by playing an "extreme" version of the game. You may want to pit two of your leaders against each other, rather than using the young people – especially if you're moving away from confectionery…You can choose what you think would be a more amusing, or extreme, substitute for marshmallows – but some contenders might include:

- Cherry tomatoes

- Popping candy

- Brussels sprouts

- Boiled eggs.

The object of the game is to get contestants to utter the words "extreme chubby bunnies" without becoming completely inaudible, or having to spit the food out! After the game, reflect on how gluttonous it was (see the Discussion Starter for another story that may help). The Bible says that our bodies are temples of the Holy Spirit (1 Corinthians 6:19), so diet and exercise, which keep our bodies healthy, are spiritual concerns. If we over-consume on a physical level, then, what does that mean on a spiritual level?

What is fasting?
(15 minutes)

Give a simple definition of today's subject: fasting. In Christian terms, it is the self-denial of something – generally food – in the pursuit of drawing closer to God.

Ask someone in the group (or several people) to read aloud Luke 4:1–15. Explain that this is perhaps the most famous example of fasting in the Bible: Jesus goes into the desert and eats nothing for forty days (so we can assume He drank water). This is a truly superhuman feat – the human body will normally shut down completely after about thirty-five days without food – and, as the passage tells us, was propelled by the Holy Spirit. Jesus seems to use this intense time to get close to His Father, God – but in doing so He also encounters the devil himself. Break into groups, and ask them to discuss the passage:

- Why do you think Jesus went without food for so long in the wilderness? Why was it necessary for Him to "fast" in this way?

- What are the results of Jesus' going without food for so long?

- Do you think Jesus really was tempted to give in and turn a stone into bread? Why or why not? And why didn't He give in?

- What do we notice in verse 1 and verse 14 (clue: it involves the Holy Spirit)? What is the significance of this?

Bring them back together, and read Acts 13:1–3. Once again, there is a dynamic connection between praying and fasting, and the movement of the Holy Spirit. Ask the group: why do you think we keep hearing about fasting and the power of the Holy Spirit together? Make sure the point is communicated that, when we pray and fast, God does something within us – and can use us – through the power of His Spirit.

The power of fasting
(15 minutes)

One of the major ways that we can fast (and one mentioned frequently in the Bible) is by abstaining from food. Obviously we can't do that to any great effect in this session – but we can agree together to begin building it into our lives in some way.

Invite a member of your church (or another Christian community) who regularly fasts as part of their spiritual life to come and speak to your group. Ask them to spend five minutes explaining what this practically involves, and what they've seen happen as a result. Then allow the group to ask questions – if none are forthcoming, you might want to guide the conversation round what it means to draw closer to God through fasting. And how does feeling hungry help us to focus on God?

After your guest has finished (you can let them go if they wish), invite everyone in the group to identify one mealtime in the week ahead that they will miss as a "fast", and to promise that they will spend the time they would have been at the meal table in prayer and devotion. Make it clear that fasting without praying (they consistently appear together in the Bible) is a bit like getting into your sports kit and then sitting on the substitute's bench for the whole match. Prayer is where the action is; fasting just leads us to the place of action.

Game: I want stuff!
(10 minutes)

Lay out magazines, catalogues and menus around your meeting room, as well as paper, glue, and scissors. Invite the young people to search through them, and cut out anything they find that they would love to have if they had unlimited financial resources. They then stick each picture onto their sheet, so that they end up with a collage of things they like and want. Once finished, get a few people to share their creations – what have they chosen and why?

Lent any time
(10 minutes)

Explain that we live in a greedy consumption culture, where advertisers are continually trying to get us not only to buy new things, but to upgrade our perfectly good old things! So we are conditioned to want more stuff – and lots of it! This applies to food, as well as to technology, clothing, music and film collections, and more. Being able to control our desires for these things is an exercise in self-discipline. Like being gluttonous with our bodies, over-consuming the things we buy and use can become a stumbling block in our relationship with God.

So, in our final activity, we're going to try to imagine that it's the beginning of Lent – the bit before Easter where we give up something for forty days – and hold our own "fast" time together. As a group you can decide whether this is going to be a week, a month, or even a full forty days, and you can choose whether to all commit to fasting from the same thing together, or fasting from different things alongside each other.

To help you decide, remember that the idea of Lent is that we deny ourselves something that can get in the way of the relationship between us and God. That might be social media websites; it might be a certain kind of food; it could be going to late-night parties, or anything else that you do too much. Agree together what the subject and duration of your fast will be – and then agree to stick to it! Pray to close the session, perhaps recapping some of the practical activities that they can take into the week ahead.

ADAPTING THE MATERIAL

For older groups... You could have a frank discussion (depending on the characters in your group) about our relationship with food, and how this affects our self-esteem. Some young people might find it easier to discuss their "friend's" struggles in this area than their own – as long as no confidences are broken and you don't get into gossip, this could be a good way of having the discussion.

For younger groups... Extend extreme chubby bunnies through the session; keep bringing back different leaders (or the same two) between activities for another round, with a different foodstuff! Make sure you have full buy-in for this from your leaders in advance!

For churchgoing young people... You could follow this up with an evening of prayer and fasting. Encourage everyone to miss dinner, and to come along to your prayer event hungry – both for food and for the power of God!

For unchurched young people... A good response at the end of the session would be to set up an office shredder, and give the young people the option of destroying their collage pictures as a way of rejecting consumerism.

Going deeper: Follow-on activities

1. SOCIAL MEDIA FAST

Five years ago, most young people had never heard of "social networking". Now, thanks to the popularity of websites such as Facebook, and before that MySpace, the phrase describes one of the key components of most teenage lives. Some young people admit to spending more time online in the average week than they do at school – to many, the digital social life is attractive and addictive in equal measure. Is this the best possible way we could be spending our time...?

Encourage as many of your group as you can to join you in a one-week social-media fast. From one week's youth meeting to the next, challenge them to leave Facebook, Twitter, instant messaging and the like behind. If you really want to ramp things up, tell them that even text messaging is for "emergency situations only"!

For some, you'll be carving a great cavernous hole in the middle of their week. To help them fill it, organize several social sessions for the week of the fast. Provide them with material for a daily devotional time – they will probably find they have time for one each day! When the week is over, congratulate and reward those who have completed it successfully, and hold a frank discussion about how it felt to take part, and what we can learn/change about ourselves as a result.

2. OVERNIGHT FAST

World Vision (www.worldvision.org.uk) run the fantastic twenty-four-hour famine initiative, a great way of raising money for those without food, while going without some for once ourselves. You could adapt the idea to raise funds for any charity, however, or you could drop the sponsorship element entirely and focus on praying and fasting together. The central idea is that you spend time together – it could be twenty-four hours; it could be just twelve or eighteen – fasting overnight. This might work as a "lock-in" at your usual youth venue, in a church, or even – with appropriate safety measures taken – outside. Make sure you spend some time having fun together, watching movies etc., but also that you pray big, risky, exciting prayers together. Perhaps construct a prayer room over the course of the evening/night, remembering that the Bible shows us that the Spirit sustains us and moves in us when we pray and fast (see Luke 4:1–15). And, of course, make sure you enjoy a hearty breakfast together the following morning!

Part Two: OUTWARD

The Public Disciplines

Week Five

Less: The Discipline of Simplicity

*"But godliness with
contentment is great gain. For
we brought nothing into
the world, and we can take
nothing out of it. But if we
have food and clothing, we will
be content with that. Those
who want to get rich fall into
temptation and a trap and
into many foolish and harmful
desires that plunge people into
ruin and destruction."*

1 Timothy 6:6–9 (TNIV)

What do you want to be when you are older? It's a question I often ask young people when I'm trying to get to know them better, because it taps directly into their hopes and their values. They usually have little hesitation in replying – even if they don't have a career in mind, there are plenty of other things they want to "be" besides an employed person. Family often comes up – particularly though not exclusively from girls; the chance to travel and "see the world" is also a popular response. In my experience, though, one thing that is on everyone's mind is money. Not necessarily the acquisition of millions – although sometimes that is *exactly* what they're aiming for. In most cases, money is a means to an end – a life of comfort, where they never have to go without the things they want. So they'll often reply that they would like a well-paid job, because without a good level of income the future perhaps seems uncomfortably uncertain.

It is my contention that modern society – certainly in Britain and America – isn't as concerned with raising young citizens as it is with creating fully-functioning economic units, capable of earning and spending plenty of money, and so keeping the wheels of capitalism spinning. The culture of consumerism is feeding them the constant lie that they will need lots of "stuff" in order to be happy, and so it is perhaps no surprise that they have worked out for themselves that money will be important in their future.

What almost never comes up when I ask that question – "What do you want to be when you're older?" – is the hope that they will retain a faith. Not because teenagers don't imagine they'll still be Christians when they get older, but perhaps because they don't spend a lot of time thinking about the future development of their faith. Rather, they are preoccupied with the things they will "need" to make their future comfortable, secure, and enjoyable. Even as they dream about the future, God gets squeezed out of the lives of young people by *stuff*.

As we begin to look now at the outward-facing Disciplines – those that we practise as individuals, but which cannot fail to make an impact on the people around us as we do so – there is none more counter-cultural than the Discipline of Simplicity. In the previous chapter, we looked at how we can pause our interactions with the gluttonous consumption culture of the West, in order to draw closer to God. In this chapter, though, we look at how we can extend moments of pause into a lifestyle that lasts a lifetime.

Simplicity is an attitude that must be both held and practised. It is a noble idea that is only proved in the way that we live. Sometimes as Christians, we do the first part of this equation really well. Just talking about a simplified life, however, has little power to transform us or the lives of those around us. If we want to see others affected by a message of simplicity, we have to live it out.

This is one of the biggest challenges for the modern church of the West. We are often quite vocal about the sins – particularly sexual sins – that we prioritize as being particularly damaging. Yet sin is sin, and as we criticize those outside the church for living a lifestyle in conflict with God's best for us, we can sometimes forget some of the apparent "lower-hierarchy" sins of which we are guilty. Money creates a particular difficulty here: although many Christians are fabulously generous with their wealth, or with their relatively meagre resources, we are a long way from the picture of the church in Acts 2, where the believers shared all they had, and where no one went without. And while generosity is important in simplicity, it is only part of the story.

Want vs need

When we look at our lives, how do we distinguish between the things that we want and the things that we need? This question can start with our possessions and resources, but it can be extended to the way that we spend our time, and even to how we invest in relationships. To a degree, the task is relatively straightforward: we don't *need* a state-of-the-art Blu-ray player but we might well *want* one; we can safely agree together that we *need* to eat food regularly. But while it is easy to discount some of our more frivolous possessions, the task soon gets harder. Do you *need* a television, for instance? As a youth worker, trying to stay abreast of youth culture in order that you might be able to connect God's story to the major stories of the modern day, not having a television might be a severe handicap.

As with everything in this book, this question is best addressed in prayer. Each of us should ask that question of God: what do I need; what do I merely want? And then a supplementary question: what are the things that I have that I don't need, but which can get in the way of my relationship with you? Finding the answers to questions such as these is the key to the Discipline of Simplicity.

As we explore this Discipline both for ourselves and with young people, we address three questions: what should I *do* less, where should I *have* less, and, perhaps surprisingly, what should I do *more*?

What should I do less?

This first question is concerned with assessing the balance of our lives. Where have we allowed the complexity of modern life, with all its work, social, church and other commitments, to overrun us? Where are we spreading ourselves too thinly? If we're always finding that there aren't enough hours in the day, this is definitely a question we need to ask ourselves. Psalm 127:2 says: "In vain you rise early and stay up late, toiling for food to eat – for he grants sleep to those he loves." Our lives aren't intended to be so full and complicated that we can barely contain them within the hours we've been given.

God is so concerned that we don't burn ourselves out with an overcomplicated lifestyle that he even included this subject in his list of Ten Commandments to the nation of Israel. And while the Sabbath day is part of the "old covenant" between God and His people, it is advocated again by the writer of Hebrews: "There remains, then, a Sabbath-rest for the people of God; for anyone who enters God's rest also rests from his own work, just as God did from his" (Hebrews 4:9–10). For youth and church workers it is of course impossible to keep Sundays (the day to which the modern world has relocated the Sabbath) free from work, but there are two Sabbath principles that I believe are important to observe.

First, the key mechanic in the Sabbath is the rhythm of six and one. This is God's ratio of "work" to "rest" – the balance observed in the creation story, and translated for our own good into the Sabbath command. It is translatable not just into the overview of our week, but into each day. The Sabbath is not about working six twenty-hour days, and then sleeping through Sunday. Each day of our lives should be well balanced. If we are awake for sixteen hours, we should be resting for at least two of them, perhaps a little more. And that word "rest" is the key here – perhaps it is helpful to define it as "time that feeds the soul." With this definition, then, most television viewing doesn't count as "rest". Time with friends might (unless you are someone who finds this deeply draining); time with God almost certainly does. Are you spending two hours each day in this kind of rest? Are the young people with whom you work? I personally find this question extremely challenging.

The second principle of Sabbath is the dedicated weekly rest day. Wisdom and experience tell us that this is simply good sense: anyone who has worked for twelve or even fourteen days without a day off will tell you how unsustainable that is; even zoo animals are given one day off from the public each week. Getting a protected rest day is particularly difficult for youth workers because we can never predict when young people might need us. It is similarly difficult to convince young people of the importance of this principle. Schoolwork generally fits around their social lives, and, at times of intense study, that can mean that they never have a day totally free of work. We should advocate strongly with young people that they have one protected day each weekend, free from work, in order to properly recharge themselves for the week ahead.

There is a third key aspect of Sabbath, but we will come to it as we ask the question, "What should I do more?"

Where should I have less?

The Discipline of Simplicity is not just concerned with how we spend our time, but also with how we expend our resources. This is where we get into one of the most difficult and potentially sacrificial areas in the whole of the Disciplines, as we assess our material possessions and try to differentiate between those that we want to have, and those that we need.

Again, the question of what "feeds the soul" is helpful here. Which of our possessions actually lead us away from either spending time with God, or walking in His ways? I'm not going to name examples because this is a question for each individual to ask of themselves and of God.

For young people, brought up in a consumerist world, this is a difficult and counter-intuitive task. The world around them is screaming at them 24/7 to buy more stuff, not to have less. Yet we have to try to help them understand that, first, riches and possessions do not make people happy (just ask any millionaire), and that, second, there is great liberation to be found in stripping away all the excess junk in our bedrooms and realizing which things are truly important to us.

Choosing to have less is, for adults and young people alike, the path to true contentment, because in doing this we are freed from the insidious snare of covetousness. Our lives become no longer about what we can get; our focus changes; the potential for our future actually opens up, because it is no longer limited by the need to earn vast sums of money. The verses at the beginning of this chapter, taken from 1 Timothy 6, tell us that "godliness with contentment", rather than a stack of snazzy possessions, is "great gain". It really is true.

I have recently experienced for myself this sense of liberation, although, if I am honest, it was not of my own choosing. My family and I realized that we were being called to move to a new area, but houses there were a lot more expensive than in the place we were leaving. We looked in vain for a house like our old one, but eventually realized that if we were going to be obedient to God and move, we would need to "downsize". This not only meant we would need to be content with less physical space (an issue given extra emphasis when my wife became pregnant again); it also had implications for our possessions. We had to leave behind my beloved sofa, which wouldn't fit into our new living room. Our dining table and chairs had to be relocated to a family garage. My music and film collections, which I'm afraid were rather bloated, had to be boxed up and put into the loft. Like ripping off a plaster, we tore the "stuff" out of our life because there was no longer room for it. We were forced to live more simply.

What do you think has been the result of that, two years on from the move? I've not become St Martin, the patron saint of simplicity, but I can honestly say that I don't miss the stuff. I used to buy a new DVD every week; now I only ever rent them. Our children haven't become frustrated at having to share a small bedroom – they love it, and have become much closer as a result. And even though we've managed to create a little more space, we have not rushed to fill it. Living more simply simply makes sense, but it's hard to believe that until you try it.

What should I do more?

The Discipline of Simplicity isn't just about stripping things out of our life, but also about asking how some of these things should be replaced. This is more a question of what we *do* than of what we *have*; a consideration again not only of what doesn't feed my soul, but also of what does. As we identify the things in our lives that are not bringing us rest, the ways in which our diaries are simply becoming too cluttered, we should also ask: what are the good things that I am not doing enough of? A simpler life allows us to prioritize these things, not to abstain from them too.

So ask that question of yourself: what is it that really feeds my soul? Good food with friends? Long walks in the country? Reading? There could be a thousand different answers. Then ask yourself: do I do enough of this? Is this how I prioritize my rest time, or do I allow it to become overrun with busyness and stuff, and then just flake out in front of the television, watching programmes about botched plastic surgery simply because they happen to be on? Many of the ways we end up spending our rest time are like the relaxation equivalent of junk food. They're easy because of the kind of world we live in, but no one would claim they're good for us.

After you've wrestled with that question for yourself, ask it of your young people. Get them to be honest with themselves about the quality of their rest time. Does it truly recharge their batteries, or does it leave them feeling tired? If the latter is true, perhaps they need to make different choices. The concept of something "feeding the soul" is perhaps going to be a little too abstract for some young people, so you could rephrase it. What things do they do that leave them feeling exhilarated, uplifted and more like the person they were created to be? What are the things they look forward to with relish and passion? Playing sport? Coming to your youth club? Going on holiday with their family?

Ultimately, the Discipline of Simplicity leads us back to God. Nothing feeds the soul like spending time with the One who made us. There is no rest to compare with that offered by Jesus (Matthew 11:28). As we declutter our lives, with respect to both what we do and what we have, and as we return to the question of what we should do more, we will inevitably find ourselves drawing closer to Him. The Discipline of Simplicity gives us freedom from the lie that we were created to rush around, work ourselves into the ground, and spend as much as we can. We were created to *be*, not to do; we were created to be with Him.

Less: Resources

First steps – The discussion starter

KEEPING IT SIMPLE

One was the daughter of a world-famous pop star; the other was heir to a hotel chain worth billions. Nicole Richie (daughter of Lionel) and Paris Hilton (who needs no introduction) were used to a lifestyle of private jets, high-class accommodation and constant pampering. They were rich, they were spoilt, and they were absolutely loving it. Then Fox TV executives came to the girls with an idea. They had come up with a format for a new reality show, in which rich girls from the city would be asked to dump the free spending, the endless possessions, and the relentless glamour, and go to live on a farm in the country. Cameras would follow them as they struggled to adapt from a life spent filing nails to one that included milking cows and shovelling pig excrement. It was to be called *The Simple Life*, and Paris and Nicole were perfect for the lead roles.

Quite why the girls agreed is open to speculation, but the show went ahead as planned. On the one hand, it was trash TV of the lowest order; on the other, it was fascinating to watch. Leaving their credit cards and mobile phones behind, the girls moved onto an Arkansas family farm, and attempted to get to grips with their new way of life. By the end of the month they had ruined the farm's milk supply, caused havoc in every area of the family business, and been politely asked to cease every task they turned their hand to.

The Simple Life ran for five years, but quickly moved away from the straightforward farm-based format that worked so well in the first season. While in one sense the show's title was intended to poke fun at the perceived intelligence of its two stars, it also reflected the simple lifestyle enjoyed by that farming family. In the light of the girls' ridiculous, tantrum-filled and utterly spoilt behaviour, the viewer was left seriously wondering whose life they would prefer to step into: the complex world of the rich socialite, or the simple hard-working life of a farmer.

Opening up

Read the story above, and then ask the following questions (you may want to show a clip from *The Simple Life* if possible):

- Which life do you think you'd rather have – that of a rich Hollywood celebrity, or that of a humble farmer? Why?

- Does money buy happiness? Why or why not?

- How would you spend your money (and your time) if you had Paris Hilton's billion-dollar fortune?

- What might be some of the most enjoyable things about farm life?

Digging deeper

- How materialistic do you think you are? Is this something you want to change (or would you just appreciate more money to spend!)?

- What are some of the possessions that you simply couldn't live without? MP3 player? Phone? Games console?

- If someone asked you to get rid of half of the 'things' you own – clothes, technology, media etc. – how easy or difficult do you think you would find it to do so?

Taking it to the word

Read 1 Timothy 6:6–10

- What do these verses suggest should be our attitude towards money and possessions?

- Note that it's the "*love of* money", not money itself, which is a root of evil. What's the distinction?

- As a practical response, consider going home and filling a bag (you can decide on the size!) with possessions you don't really need and – with parental permission – taking them to a charity shop.

- How else could you declutter or simplify your life?

The adaptable meeting guide

Meeting aim: To introduce the idea that living simply is a part of the Christian life that effectively mirrors the way Jesus lived; to help young people to identify the difference between those things they want and those they need.

Before you start: You will need cards with the names of the story sagas for the first activity; pens – for writing and for drawing – and paper; flip-chart paper and pen. You might wish to buy cheap, blank journal-style books if you are working with churchgoing young people (see **Adapting the Material**).

Game: keep it simple
(15 minutes)

Split into teams – giving a nominated leader from each team one of the following well-known story titles. Make sure that the team contains at least one person who is familiar with the main arc of the story they are given:

- *The Lord of the Rings*

- *The Bible*

- *The "Star Wars" Trilogies*

- *The History of the World from 1900 onwards*

- *Friends (series 1–10)*

- *Other epic stories with which they will be familiar.*

Explain that the team has five minutes to simplify the entire story – with all the major plot twists and turns – into a maximum one-minute dramatic performance (shorter if possible). After answering any questions, give them five minutes to create and rehearse their skits, then get everyone to perform to the rest of the group. Afterwards, explain that this session is all about the Christian Discipline of Simplicity – by which we simplify our over-complicated lives.

When I'm older
(10 minutes)

Gather the whole group together, and ask each person to briefly sum up their hopes for the future. What do they want to be, do and have when they grow up? Expect to hear answers like the following:

- *Good job*

- *Lots of money*

- *Travelling and seeing the world*

- *Attractive / funny / rich spouse(!)*

When everyone has spoken, note how many of them have mentioned the idea of a more mature relationship with God as part of their future. It is unlikely that this will be a priority for many. For most, the ability to accumulate more "stuff" will be much higher on the agenda. If this is indeed how the group has responded, ask them why they think that is.

Want vs need
(10 minutes)

Write the following list on flip-chart paper in a prominent place in your venue: iPad; iPhone; Bible; Laptop; Blu-ray player and films; Christian music collection; HDTV; Designer clothes collection; Latest PlayStation/Xbox; Mountain bike. Explain: you are given all ten of these items, but are then told that you have to get rid of five. So which do you keep? They now have two minutes to write a list of the ones they will keep. Feed back, then repeat the activity – but this time they have to get the list down to only two. Again, give them two minutes to do this, then feed back. As they do, ask them to explain how they arrived at their answer. How would they feel about life without the other eight items? Open the Bible, and read 1 Timothy 6: 6–10 to the group. Ask:

- *What do these verses seem to suggest about how much "stuff" we should have as Christians?*

- *What are some of the things that you have, over and above "food and clothing", that you feel are vital to your contentment?*

- *How can we decide the difference between the things we need to be content, and the things we "foolishly desire"?*

- *How can our possessions – and the quest for more – "plunge people into ruin and destruction?"*

Say: this passage seems to suggest that there are some things we need, which are good for us, and some things we want, which perhaps aren't. This session is about simplifying our lives so that we have all of the first category, and care less about the second.

Where should
I have less?
(10 minutes)

Give out coloured pens and paper. In groups, ask the young people to draw a diagrammatic picture of their bedroom, complete with all their valued possessions. Make sure they make these as detailed as possible, and annotate them with all their major possessions (they don't need to list individual items – "DVD collection" or "Clothes" is fine). As they sketch, encourage them to show each other what they are drawing, and to talk about their favourite "things".

After they have beautified the drawings, ask them to go through their "room" with a (preferably red) pen, and draw a large circle around the things that they honestly feel they need in order to be content. Next, they should strike a large cross through everything else. Get some feedback. What did they choose to keep? What did they delete? Would they consider actually removing one or more of these items from their life? What might be the result if they did?

What should I do less?
(10 minutes)

Read Psalm 127:2. Ask: do you feel that you have enough time to do everything you need to? Do you get enough sleep?

Get everyone to write the number "24" at the top of a piece of paper. This is (obviously) the number of hours we get each day, and we spend at least some of them in the way that we choose. Ask them to subtract from this the number of hours they spend at school or work each day, and then the number of hours they spend asleep on an average night. They should be left with a number around eight. As you read the following list, ask them to subtract from that number the number of hours they spend on an average day engaged in that activity.

- *Homework / coursework*

- *Sports, clubs and societies*

- *Time on the Internet*

- *Time spent devoted to mobile phone*

- *Meals*

- *Showering and cleaning self*

- *Watching TV / films*

- *Doing things that "feed the soul": e.g. quiet times, reading, going for walks, etc.*

Before long, some of the young people may hit zero, even though they also do many of the other things on the list. Say that we all do so much, and many of us apparently do more than time allows. In groups, ask them to decide which things from this list they should be doing less of, and which they should perhaps leave more time for.

What could I do more?
(10 minutes)

Read Hebrews 4:9–10 to introduce the concept of Sabbath and rest. Break into pairs – ideally placing good, same-sex friends together – and set each person the task of talking for just thirty seconds about the things that "feed their soul". What are the things they do at rest which, when they start to do them, make them come alive? After both have spoken, encourage them to be honest with each other about how much they do these things.

If (as is likely) they don't spend nearly enough of their time involved in truly restful activity, then they are disobeying God's command to them to rest (part of the Ten Commandments, but restated in Hebrews above so that we're in no doubt that it still applies!) This command comes not out of God's desire to order us around, but because He cares so much for us that He doesn't want to see us burning ourselves out or running on empty.

For the week ahead, then, everyone in the room will have an accountability partner whose job it is to check that they're getting enough good-quality rest. Encourage everyone not only to do much more in the next week that "feeds their soul", but also to check up on one another and spur each other on – with the threat that next week that you'll begin the session by checking how everyone got on!

ADAPTING THE MATERIAL

For older groups… They may not want to do a drama activity (the opening game), so you could simplify this into a storytelling game, where the group leader has to tell the entire story of the relevant epic in just one minute or less.

For younger groups... The final task, and particularly the question of "what feeds your soul" might be a bit abstract for some. If so, get them talking about how they spend their weekends, and encourage them to agree together an amount of time that they will spend disconnected from the Internet, away from their phone, and not watching TV or playing video games.

For churchgoing young people... Focus much more on the idea of making dedicated devotional time each day. Could they begin a devotional journal, where they start to record their prayers and Bible readings? You could give out cheap blank journals for this purpose.

For unchurched young people... Don't expect them to know the story of the Bible, and read fewer of the Bible references to justify your arguments. Argue that the rest rhythm of six and one simply makes good sense – ask for their opinions and reflections on that. From experience, how much rest do they think they need?

Going deeper: Follow-on activities

1. WANT VS NEED

This exercise gives young people a chance to create a "wish list" – and then analyse its true worth. Give out pens and paper, and allow your group ten minutes (they can talk to each other during this time) to come up with a comprehensive list of the things they would buy if, right now, you handed them a million pounds. How much of it would they spend, save or invest? How much of it would they give away, and to whom would they give it? What are the essential and luxury items they'd love to get their hands on?

Get a few of the group to read out their lists. Now, in the context of the Discipline of Simplicity, get them to go through the list, asking this question of each item: is this something I *want* or something I *need*? They should put a line through anything that falls into the first category. Now ask those people who read their original lists to read out the edited versions. Hold a discussion based on that central question of *want vs need*. How do we decide the difference? And what impact could this have on the way we live our lives, and on the amount we give away to others?

2. FACEBOOK DETOX

Working on the assumption that all your young people have a) social networking profiles and b) mobile devices on which they can access them, ask everyone in your group to log on at the same time (alternatively, this might work best as something for them to go away and do in their own time after the session on simplicity). Explain that you are going to go through a social networking detox together – not giving it up, but giving it a much-needed spring clean. The challenge to them is to rid their social networking (e.g. Facebook) profiles of:

- *Extra personal information that could be unsafe and shouldn't be viewable online*

- *"Friends" whom they have added but don't actually know in person*

- *Favourite quotes, etc. that don't reflect well on them as Christians*

- *Extraneous applications (perhaps involving online farming) which clutter up their online experience, and that of their friends!*

After they have completed the exercise, make sure you catch up with them, either as a group or as individuals, to find out how easy/difficult it was, and to explore what the effects of these steps might be.

Week Six

Alone: The Discipline of Solitude

"Jesus often withdrew to lonely places and prayed."

Luke 5:16

I'm no fan of my own company. In fact, based on how bored I get when spending time with myself, it's a wonder that I've managed to find friends who will put up with me. My natural instinct when left alone at home is to switch on the television, grab the phone, check my email, log on to Facebook – anything to dispel the sensation of being alone. When silence falls, I run loudly in the opposite direction. My life is too full of noise and distraction for me to be suddenly plunged into the depths of quiet solitude. I am so used to perpetual motion that it feels unnatural to stop.

As I read these honest reflections back, they do not seem healthy. If I were psycho-analysing myself, I might suggest I was running from something. The fear of silence, perhaps, or rather the fear of the power that it contains. When I genuinely stop, slow down my racing mind, and allow myself to be quiet and still, I invariably find that God invades my thoughts. So, as I run away from silence, am I really running away from God?

Listening

I still remember my parents telling me that God had given me two ears and one mouth. Then, a very strange old French teacher, frustrated that I was extremely talkative except when it came to speaking French, hammered the following rhyme so deep into my psyche that I have no difficulty recounting it twenty years later:

A wise old owl lived in an oak;
The more he saw, the less he spoke;
The less he spoke, the more he heard;
Why can't we all be like that wise old bird?

At the time we thought it faintly ridiculous, and told her so in no uncertain terms (she left the school soon afterwards, citing behavioural problems in certain classes). However, since then, I have begun to reflect on this old poem with both nostalgia and regret. Experience has taught me that the moral is a good one – when we stop speaking and start to listen, we stand at the beginning of wisdom. Or something about how we should all live in a tree (maybe I've missed the point).

When we think about our personal relationship with God, I wonder how much it reflects the principle of the wise old owl. When we pray, how much time do we spend doing the talking, and for how long do we listen out for the reply? If I'm honest, I know that I am much happier in the role of speaker than of listener. So much of my spiritual life is about self-generated input – the prayers I say, the books and Bible passages I choose to read – that I know I don't leave much space for God's part in our relationship. I'm so busy that perhaps time spent "doing nothing", simply waiting on God, can feel like a waste.

If there is a silence in our time with God, it is a discipline in itself not to break or fill it ourselves. There is willpower and restraint involved in simply maintaining quiet; in listening instead of speaking or grabbing something with which to busy ourselves. We have already looked at how difficult it is in our culture to slow down the frenetic pace of our lives and stop for any significant amount of time. Arguably the task of simply listening in those times is a greater challenge still. Yet how can we expect to hear from God if we are not taking the time to listen for His voice?

When the Lord appears to Elijah in 1 Kings 19, we see a fabulous picture both of the awesome majestic power of God and of the nature of His voice. He tells Elijah to go and stand on Horeb, the "mountain of God", because He is about to pass by:

> Then a great and powerful wind tore the mountains apart and shattered the rocks before the Lord, but the Lord was not in the wind. After the wind there was an earthquake, but the Lord was not in the earthquake. After the earthquake came a fire, but the Lord was not in the fire. And after the fire came a gentle whisper. When Elijah heard it, he pulled his cloak over his face and went out and stood at the mouth of the cave.
> (1 Kings 19:11–13)

What do these verses, and this picture of God, say to you? God is capable of both putting on the ultimate Earth, Wind and Fire gig (not my finest contemporary pop-culture reference, I know) and being present in a gentle whisper. Ultimate power and ultimate calm; side by side; simultaneous. Our lives are loud and busy, certainly more earthquake than calm. I am challenged by this picture: do I spend enough time listening for the still, small voice of God? The voice that speaks in a "gentle whisper"? The Spiritual Discipline of Solitude, the practice of silence and listening for the voice of God in that silence, is a way of addressing this imbalance in all our lives.

The power of solitude

Simply put, the Discipline of Solitude is the act of taking ourselves out of the busyness of everyday life, of seeking God in the silence of retreat. It is not necessarily about physically separating ourselves from the world, but choosing to do so can generally be helpful as we take our hearts and minds into a place of quiet reflection.

Spiritual solitude is not loneliness. This is what we fear when we enter into it; if we're honest this fear can keep us from it. Yet when we choose to be alone with God, we are far from alone. He – with the power of an earthquake but the voice of a whisper – is intimately present with us; in my experience He can draw significantly closer to us when we take the step of separating ourselves from other people; from the busyness of everyday life.

I have a rather more sporadic approach to retreat time than I would like, but when the chance arises I usually grab it with both hands. When I have done this, the experience has often been remarkable. Reading through the notes I have made on silent retreats, I am staggered by the significant ways in which I believed God was speaking to me during those times. By shutting my own mouth, taking myself out of my normal context, and freeing myself from the clutches of work, phone, television, and a hundred other distractions, I have created the space for God to speak. There is no magic formula, no method by which we can conjure up His presence – the experience of thousands of Christians through the ages simply tells us that when we are silent, God speaks.

On one occasion a few years ago, I spent a day in silence close to my home. I had intended to spend the whole time in a quiet local chapel, but after a couple of hours I felt prompted to go for a walk. I had relaxed into the pace of the day – a world away from what I'm used to – and had begun to tune in just a little to that guiding voice.[9] Still in silence, I went on one of the longest walks of my life, so far in fact that at the end of the day I had to make a significant journey home. During that walk, I believe that my attention was drawn to certain things; as I wrote my thoughts in a journal, it seemed as if they were being shaped in some way. By the end of a lengthy journey, I had clearly been directed through the day, clearly been the recipient of guidance. For once I had shut up for a few hours and made space for God. He filled the silence.

---

9 What do I mean by that? Not an audible voice certainly, but a sense within my own mind that my thoughts were being guided. I have only heard an audible voice which I would attribute to God himself once in my life; most of the time I simply believe that when my thoughts are focused on Him, He is in the midst of my thinking.

Solitude and young people

How confident are you that you can "sell" the idea of silence and solitude to today's super-connected teenagers? Just as with all the Spiritual Disciplines, I genuinely believe that young people rise to meet our level of expectation. If we don't think they'll be able to cope with silent reflection, they almost certainly won't be able to – they will pick up in the way that we present ideas and activities an assumption that this is beyond them. If, however, we show that we believe they are mature enough to cope with something like silence, they will live up to that.

The way into the Discipline for young people – and for the rest of us too – is not the deep end of a forty-eight-hour silent retreat. There are steps into solitude that ease us into a habit of listening more than we speak.

It starts small. We need first of all to learn – adults and young people alike – to enjoy little opportunities for silence. This in itself is counter-cultural; there are so many devices and profiles and accounts for us to check that we can fill every second of our lives with communication and media. Whereas in the past a train journey, a five-minute wait at a bus stop, even the first moments of the day between waking and rising, would have been moments of enforced quiet, now they can be filled with unimportant Things-To-Do. So, as we step into the Discipline of Solitude, the first thing to do is to reclaim these opportunities for pause in each day. This might mean making deliberate choices: not having a mobile device next to our bed; forcing ourselves not to call a friend if we find ourselves out for a walk. Instead of constantly using these moments to plug in to the social world, we can begin to use them to acknowledge our continuous relationship with God. This ongoing need for activity and communication can otherwise begin to crowd Him out of our lives. Simply making a commitment to use moments of pause in this way can immediately strengthen our connection with and ability to listen to God.

The next step is to begin to discover for ourselves a place where we can be quiet and, preferably, undisturbed. For those of us not living under our parents' roof this is potentially easier; some of us even have the benefit of a study (I don't; I'm writing this on the floor of my living room). Finding a designated quiet place, preferably one that is free of too many tempting distractions, is important if we want to try to build longer periods of quiet contemplation into our lives. The absolute ideal would be a well-lit, heated and comfortable room containing little more than somewhere to sit, since this will work as a year-round venue; we might also choose to find an outdoor space, perhaps in a local park, where we are unlikely to be disturbed. There is a balance to be struck here between seclusion and safety – we should not ask young people to take themselves off alone into the depths of the woods, for instance. Once we have found a quiet place, the next challenge is to carve out time to spend there. When we do, we should take nothing that might distract us, save perhaps for a Bible, journal and pen.

There is not very much to say about what to do in this quiet place. In essence, we should do nothing, although of course this is impractical – our God-given minds cannot simply be switched off. Instead, then, we should make the decision to continually hit the reset button on our wandering brain, trying to simply enjoy the chance of stillness and listening out for the voice of God – whether truly audible or as an overpowering sensation of guidance inside us.

After we have begun to build up our silence and listening muscles, there is a third step to take – silent retreat. A full day, or even more, spent with the simple aim of quietly listening for the voice of God. This is a big leap from our regular way of life, and while it will be easier for the introvert than the extrovert, it is achievable for both if built up to through the first two steps.

A retreat should again take place in a comfortable but humble place. There should most definitely not be an Internet connection. Others would adopt a more pure approach, but personally I would advocate taking along a couple of quite diverse books – perhaps a commentary and a book of poetry, for instance – for study and meditation during the day. A retreat is a place where all the inward Disciplines come together; to my mind at least it is not solely about being silent and constantly trying to clear the mind to discern God. Solitude sets the *context* for retreat, but there is space for the other Disciplines to be practised too.

A retreat can take many forms; here is just one suggestion of how to run one with young people. Make a day or overnight booking at a small residential centre, for a small group of young people (plus appropriate leaders) who have already been introduced to the first two steps. Divide your time together into slots, including times to share simple food, and at least one opportunity to enjoy an act of corporate worship. The majority of the slots are then allocated to times of quiet, where the young people each find a quiet place and spend (a minimum of) an hour at a time in solitude: listening, reading, praying, and working through resources that you may have given them.

Encourage (safe) ventures outdoors; proximity to nature can be inspirational. I would also suggest that, if you're staying overnight, you promote the idea of a long, healthy sleep. For many young people this just isn't prioritized, despite all the silly media stereotypes. With mobile phones, games consoles, televisions and more to distract them, teenagers (like adults) are often guilty of neglecting their need for good sleep.

In your communal time, take the risk of asking deep questions. What did they "hear" when they listened to God? What doubts have arisen for them? Use some of this time to help them to think through with you what the retreat time has meant to them. Agree promises together about how you'd all like daily life to change as a result of this retreat. The time shouldn't be solemn or (as we all fear) boring. We should have high expectations of them and of God that their time in quiet will be anything but dull. You should also take time to relax and have fun in low-tech ways; you could make a feature of getting hold of some old-fashioned board games and playing them together in the evening.

At the end of your time together you should all be able to say that you have spent time with God and slowed down, but also crucially that you have enjoyed yourselves. How else would we expect anyone who attended to bring these elements of solitude into their everyday life?

Why outward?

A quick note on why Solitude is classified as an outward, public Discipline. Of course, the act of setting ourselves apart and being quiet is a practice of the inner life, but it affects others in at least two ways.

First, since we live as part of a community and/or family, our disappearance will be noted. Jesus practised solitude; as we noted earlier, He often "retreated" whenever His ministry became intense. To return to Luke 5, where we learn (verse 16) that "Jesus often withdrew to lonely places and prayed", we see a context of crowds, desperately clamouring for His teaching and His healing power. The disciples themselves had only just been called; they themselves would have been wondering where on earth He kept disappearing to. Not only that; they had to explain His disappearance – like that of some reclusive celebrity – to His "fans" at the very height of His popularity. Solitude takes us out of everyday life, and leaves a noticeable hole, which both encourages others to take similar action and prompts those who do not know God to ask questions of our motivation.

Secondly, Solitude affects others, because when we are practising silence and listening we cannot fail to be transformed through sheer exposure to God. We are more in tune with His heart for the world; we naturally become more gentle, sensitive and caring. The act of flexing our listening muscles then makes us a better listener in our conversations; we are less distracted, distractible, fidgety, agitated. Solitude helps us to deprogram some of the junk that modern life puts into us, and the process not only changes us for the better, but has a ripple effect on those around us.

Alone: Resources

First steps – The discussion starter

100 YEARS IN SOLITARY

They were locked up in a time when inequality and racism were still rife; they sat forgotten for decades. Three men, jailed in solitary cells in an American prison for the alleged murder of a guard, endured almost unimaginable psychological torture for a combined total of over 100 years.

In 1972, three African–American inmates of Louisiana's Angola prison were convicted of the murder of one of their guards – a charge they still deny to this day. The men – Robert Hillary King, Albert Woodfox and Herman Wallace – had previously become known in the prison as a force for good. They had staged peaceful protests for better conditions, and organized a culture of respect and honour among the inmates which had dramatically improved behaviour inside the jail. In a strange way, through non-violence in a violent world, they had become powerful – and this, plus their links to political guerrilla group the Black Panthers, also made them dangerous. When their conviction for the guard's murder was initially announced, there was great uproar; time passed, however, and the men – who became known as the Angola Three – were forgotten by the outside world.

It was not until 1997, when a former Black Panther member and a law student decided to reinvestigate the case, that it came to light that all three men had spent the last twenty-five years of their lives in solitary confinement. To be clear: they weren't together; they were completely alone. They had been taken out of the general prison population and placed in small, individual, maximum-security cells.

After twenty-nine years in solitary King was released, having seen his original charge reduced. At time of writing, Woodfox and Wallace – who still protest their innocence – are still in Angola prison. In 2008, after huge international pressure, the men were finally taken out of solitary and placed with other prisoners. They had each been in solitary for thirty-six years.

Opening up

Read the story above, and then ask the following questions:

- How does this story make you feel?

- If the men are guilty of the murder of a guard (they deny this), do you think this could be considered a just punishment?

- For what reasons might the prison authorities have decided to put these three men in these conditions for so long?

- Is there any practical way that you can become involved in the cause of the Angola Three or others like them?

Digging deeper

- How would you feel about spending a year in solitary confinement? What about a month? A week? A day?

- How do you think prolonged time in solitary might affect you?

- Might there be some positive outcomes and changes? What might these be?

- How often are you alone? How easy or difficult do you find it to cut yourself off from other people?

Taking it to the word

Read Luke 5:12–16

- What do you think about Jesus' behaviour here? Just as He's getting famous – He seems to run away! Why?

- What does the fact that Jesus "often withdrew to *lonely* places" say to you?

- What does this imply for those who might choose to follow Jesus?

- Think back to anything that you thought might be a positive outcome of being placed in solitary confinement. How might voluntarily placing ourselves there occasionally be spiritually good for us?

The adaptable meeting guide

Meeting aim: To reflect on the "noise" that fills our everyday lives, and help young people to engage with silence not as a punishment but as a much-needed escape from the non-stop social and academic pressures of life.

Before you start: <u>If at all possible, do not hold this meeting in your normal venue.</u> Instead, try to find a reverent space that lends itself to quiet, solitary reflection. A church sanctuary would be perfect – if you don't have access to an old church building, there may be one in your locality that will happily allow you to come and visit – or at the right time of year the session could work well in an outdoor space (you will need to adapt some of the activities if so). To run the session you will need strong material strips for the three-legged runners, and enough Bibles to share one between two.

Three legs vs two (5 minutes)

What better way to illustrate that sometimes it's better to run the race on your own than with this game? Ask the young people to raise their hands if they are either a) very fast, good runners, or b) very slow, unsporty types (you're not interested in the average ones here). Being careful to protect any feelings, set up a race involving two of the best runners and two of the worst, and explain that you're going to conduct a 50m dash (if space allows). Ask the rest of the group who they think will win. Just before you start, produce your strips of material, and tie the legs of the two best runners together, but leaving the two slower runners unrestricted. Then start the race. With no practice, the faster runners will certainly lose.

Explain that, in this session, we're going to explore why, sometimes, it's better to go it alone.

Introducing solitude
(5 minutes)

Explain: in this session, we're going to look at the Spiritual Discipline of Solitude – which is about taking ourselves away from the busyness of our lives and silently giving God space to speak to us. It is about being alone, but not loneliness; about silence, but not emptiness; about listening, not just hearing. This session will include an opportunity to be silent, and, unlike in the exercises we did for the Discipline of Meditation, do absolutely nothing.

Split into groups, and ask them to discuss the following questions:

- Do you enjoy your own company?

- How often do you make space to be alone? How often do you truly do nothing?

- How much do you hear from God? Do you think you might hear from Him more if you created more space to listen to Him?

  And crucially…

- How do you feel about the idea that, in this session, you'll be asked to do nothing for fifteen minutes?

Do nothing but listen
(7 minutes)

Ask everyone to find a space in the venue where they can still hear you. Get them to switch off phones (ideally, they'll have handed them in at the door, but this might be impractical!) and other distractions, and explain that, for just three or four minutes, you'll be asking them to be completely silent. Before they start, though, ask them what they can hear. Make sure you don't ask that question when the venue is already silent, but when there is still a gentle hubbub of conversation. They may pick up some sounds nearby, but they will generally tell you that they can't hear very much.

Ask them to relax, and to be completely silent for a few minutes. Then begin to slowly read the following:

Be still. Notice your breathing, and begin to slow it down, taking long, deep breaths. Make yourself completely comfortable. Relax your body. Allow yourself to be completely silent.

(pause)

Now, listen. What can you hear? Not just here, but further away. What is happening outside? Your ears are very powerful; if you listen, you can pick up sounds that are a long way away. Take just a couple of minutes to do nothing except listen.

After two more minutes, gently regain the focus of the group. Remind them of what they said they could hear when you started; now ask them: were they able to hear more by taking part in the listening activity? The point should be obvious to them: if we want to really hear things, sometimes we have to truly stop and listen. But why is that relevant to us as Christians?

A gentle whisper
(10 minutes)

Set a little of the background context to the story of Elijah on Mount Horeb (he is a prophet of God; he has just proved that the Lord is God on Mount Carmel, and then slaughtered the prophets of the fake god Baal; now he's on the run from the angry royal family).

Ask a dramatically gifted member of the group (or one of the leaders) to perform a reading of 1 Kings 19:1–13b. Ask the group:

- What are the messages we hear in this passage (particularly verses 11–13) about the power of God, and the presence (or voice) of God?

- Are these conflicting and contradictory, or somehow complementary images of God?

- What does this passage show us about how we can hear from God? How could developing our abilities as listeners help us to hear Him better sometimes?

Listen to me
(10 minutes)

Ask the young people to pair up – ideally with someone they don't know well. Tell everyone that they now have thirty seconds to tell their partner about everything that has happened to them today, from the moment they woke up until now. The catch? They both have to speak at once. Give them little warning, and start the activity. When the thirty seconds are up, pick on a few pairs to see if either can give an accurate retelling of the other person's day. It's unlikely that most will gather much information (although I have uncovered strangely gifted people through running this activity!).

Now repeat the activity – choosing another subject if you wish (such as all the TV shows you've seen this week) – but this time they can speak consecutively, rather than at the same time. Again, pick on a few to feed back; the results ought to be much better. Again, the lesson is simple: it's great to talk in relationships – and if we never talk, the relationship doesn't develop much. It's the same with our prayer life. But relationships – both earthly and spiritual – are not about a one-way conversation. Sometimes we need to stop and listen to the other person.

Retreat!
(20 minutes)

For the rest of the session, you're going to tackle the big one – a full fifteen minutes of silence. Before you start, bring the group together and ask them how they feel about the prospect of this period of solitude. They may feel bored even by the thought of it; they may even feel nervous. Try to put their minds at rest by telling them that there is no wrong way to do this activity – as long as they don't disturb anyone else, and remain silent. If they close their eyes and fall asleep, that's OK too! The idea of the activity is to rest in the presence of God, and that means truly relaxing.

Invite them all to find a space, to switch off distractions, and

143

to remove watches or anything else that will tell them the time. If at all possible, remove or cover any clocks in the space. Now say a quick prayer, asking God to speak to everyone, and ask them to relax, quiet themselves, and listen out for the "gentle whisper" of God's voice.

At the end of fifteen minutes, offer them the chance to move into a non-quiet space. If, however, some wish to remain in silence, try to support this for a few more minutes. Afterwards, make sure you and your other leaders catch up informally with all the young people who have taken part in the session, to see how they found their time in silence.

ADAPTING THE MATERIAL

For older groups... You may wish to find your own, simpler words for the "do nothing but listen" activity, rather than reading the words prepared. Perhaps explain the concept in advance, and then let them find their own way. Also, you may feel some older groups are ready for an even longer period of solitude than fifteen minutes!

For younger groups... Reduce the amounts of time for the various silences, in line with what you think your group can handle. They will, however, live up (or down) to your expectations of them; they should still be able to manage eight to ten minutes of silence in the final activity.

For churchgoing young people... Extend the Bible study on 1 Kings 19. Split into groups, and look more at the first half of the passage. What else do we learn about the character and patience of God in the first ten verses?

For unchurched young people... You know your group best – assess how they'll feel about the Retreat activity at the end of session. This *could* be a great opportunity for them to open up to hearing from God; for some the "do nothing but listen" activity will have been quite enough silence for one day!

Going deeper: Follow-on activities

1. BACK TO THE CENTRE

This is a simple technique with which to arm young people who might find silence and listening difficult. When we try to listen for the voice of God, even the most disciplined among us can get distracted and sidetracked. One minute, we're quietly listening out; the next we're reliving that episode of *CSI* we watched the previous evening (and it is unlikely that God is speaking through *that*). To be able to explain this one effectively, you should probably try it out for yourself. So, when you come to your place of quiet, think of a word or phrase that is special to your relationship with God, and which will help you to focus on God. It might be something like: "God, You have my full attention"; I always use the phrase (for reasons I won't go into now): "God, You are my director."

Now, as you wait on God in the silence, and as distractions inevitably come, quietly repeat your chosen phrase, perhaps three times. You should find that your attention has shifted back to the place where you wanted it to be. Use the phrase as often as you need it – in my experience it's a great tool for maintaining a listening focus on God. Just one note: my flippant comment about *CSI* might be unhelpful; we shouldn't block off any avenue through which God might be seeking to speak to us. Memories, bits of conversations that we haven't processed properly, and, yes, even plot points we've remembered from last night's television show *could* be a channel for the voice of God. A key part of the process of listening is discernment, and we should keep praying for it in abundance as we practise this Discipline.

2. WRITING RETREAT

Encourage those young people who enjoy writing and reflecting to take an hour with a journal – perhaps at the bottom of a garden, or in some other safe outdoor space – to spend in silence. As they listen for the voice of God, they should write down *everything* that comes into their head – even if some of it seems frivolous or irrelevant. At the end of the hour they – with your help if they ask for it – can go through what they have written, and reflect on what God may have been saying to them. This is a great way of showing young people that, far from being dull, silent contemplation produces a great number of thoughts, even in just one hour.

Week Seven

Last: The Discipline of Submission

"Submit to one another out of reverence for Christ."

Ephesians 5:21

There are few words that contain the power to stir up controversy in the church as greatly as "submission". Arguments about the rights and wrongs of male headship have the power to split entire communities. Biblical mentions of submission have in the past been used to legitimize the slave trade. Tyrannical, abusive church leaders have been allowed to continue in leadership dysfunction in the name of submission.

Happily, this is not what biblical submission is all about. In fact, being *right* and winning arguments is the very last thing it's about. In Mark 9:35, Jesus calls the Twelve together and tells them: "If anyone wants to be first, he must be the very last, and servant of all." I think that's a brilliant piece of wording – not just last, but *the very last*. This is what it means to follow Jesus – this is what it means to "take up [our] cross daily and follow" Him (Luke 9:23). The Spiritual Discipline of Submission is all about becoming the very last, and servant of all.

The freedom of submission

We, like many of our young people, may perceive the idea of submission as a negative thing – perhaps because of some of the abuses mentioned above. We may think of it from the perspective of being oppressed, or ruled over. Yet submission isn't about oppression; it's actually about freedom.

When we submit to others, we are freed from the consumerist lie that it is always right to have things our own way. We are freed from the proud pursuit of always having to be right; the implicit belief that our opinions and ideas count double because they're *ours*. Submission takes our focus off ourselves – and self-obsession can be a tiring pursuit. It is liberating to live for others; to take our own interests off the top spot on the day's agenda.

Today's teenagers have grown up in a society in which this idea is entirely counter-cultural. The idea that you shouldn't get your own way is entirely alien to a consumerist, individualist world view. Modern pluralism tells us that somehow we can *all be right*, as long as our beliefs don't encroach on anyone else's. The wisdom of this world calls this freedom – but is that really what it is?

The Discipline of Submission teaches young people about the true freedom that comes in not allowing ourselves to become god. It leads them towards humility, encouragement, contentment and love. It is an outward Discipline, but it is also in many ways a communal one – because submission really comes to life in a community, such as that described in Acts 2, where everyone is putting themselves last. This must be our aim as we cultivate

Christian community among young people – to form groups who function in submission to one another.

Foster's seven acts of submission

In *Celebration of Discipline*, Richard Foster describes seven "acts" of submission, which function as good markers for us on the road to submission. In cultivating the Discipline of Submission in young people, we can point them towards living in submission:

- **To God:** We are no longer ours but His. When we are born again (John 3:3), we die to the old self and its associated inward focus. Submission means being able to say to God: I'll go where You want me to go, not just in the big things, such as where I choose to live or work, but in the minutiae of every day.

- **To the Bible:** Submitting to God means also submitting to His word. This doesn't mean we have to simply swallow unthinkingly every interpretation of Scripture (as we know, these range wildly); it means making a lifelong commitment to reading and – through the intervention of the Spirit – understanding the Bible better, so that we might then be informed in every decision about the way of God. See Week Two for more detail on this.

- **To our family:** Upwards, sideways, downwards. We submit to our parents as we honour them, just as God commands Moses. We submit to our wives and husbands out of reverence for Christ, and thus look to "die" for one another in the way that

149

He ultimately loved the church. We submit to our children if we have them, because we are no longer the centre point or focus of our own family life.

- **To our neighbours:** True community is about sharing so that no one goes without. It is about stepping out of the isolation of our own homes, and recognizing that we should "do life" with the people alongside whom we live. For young people that may not mean a geographical neighbourhood, but the community of school or college. It can sometimes be very challenging to put our peers first; competitiveness and selfishness are keenly felt in a school environment. Submission challenges us to find another way – and what an extraordinary witness it creates.

- **To the church:** This can be a hard sell for adults, let alone young people! And perhaps when we view it simply as an institution, rather than as a body of people, it can in some cases seem difficult to "submit" to the church. Yet the church is an intrinsic part of God's rescue plan for the world, and we must learn to submit to it. Giving ourselves, and our resources to the local church – even when we don't agree with every matter of style or policy – is a vital aspect of the Discipline of Submission.

- **To the broken:** The Bible is literally overflowing with references to the poor, and to the imperative for God-followers to serve them. The aid agency World Vision commissioned researchers to produce a "Poverty and Justice" Bible, with relevant verses highlighted – they claimed to find over 2,000 references to the subject. This is perhaps the most intuitive application of Jesus' command for us to become "the very last" – we are even to submit ourselves to those the world would value least of all.

- **To the world:** In one of the most extraordinary passages in the New Testament, John 13:1–17, Jesus washes the feet of His disciples. This is not about who they are – it is all about who He is. Jesus, who is fully God, stoops to clean the disgusting (and they would have been) filthy feet of humble men. And just in case we don't understand the application, He spells it out, which is interesting in itself because He rarely does so. Verses 14 and 15 really underline the point: "Now that I, your Lord and Teacher, have washed your feet, you also should wash one another's feet. I have set you an example that you should do as I have done for you." Jesus really wants us to understand that this picture is for us to replicate. So for all of us, young and old, the Discipline of Submission requires us to ask: what does it mean to wash the feet of the world?

In the light of the cross

The Discipline of Submission is perhaps so compelling because, more than any of the others, it points to and models the way of the crucified Christ. It requires us to ask what it really means to live out Jesus' words in Luke 9: "If anyone would come after me, he must deny himself and take up his cross daily and follow me." Submission is about following – even in leadership – through listening, sacrificing, and serving. It is a commitment to John 3:30: He must become greater; I must become less. The practical way we work this out is not simply in how we love Him, but in how we love one another.

Submission leads naturally into the next Discipline that we will look at: Service. One naturally leads to the other, but while Service is mainly about practice, Submission is perhaps mainly about heart attitude. If we help young people to grow in the Discipline of Submission, we will be assisting them in developing an attractive, wise and Christ-like character.

Last: Resources

First steps – The discussion starter

A HUMBLING EXPERIENCE

Lisa was twenty-seven years old when she made the decision to leave her well-paid job in business to work for a missionary organization. She believed that God was calling her to work for Operation Mobilisation, a charity that sails former ocean liners to deprived parts of the world to offer medical help, Christian teaching and other services. She was posted to the *Doulos*, one of the organization's "mercy ships", and quickly given her first assignment on board: in the kitchen.

It was quite a leap from the trendy corporate lifestyle Lisa was used to. She had previously been making important decisions on behalf of major clients; now she was peeling potatoes to be served to the ship's lowly guests. There was an even bigger shock, though – her "boss" in this new role was an eighteen-year-old girl; one who had never held a job before and clearly didn't know what she was doing.

Lisa had a decision to make: should she overrule this poor confused girl and take over, knowing that her general level of capability was much higher, or should she somehow submit to the authority this girl had been given? She searched her soul, and realized that if she truly believed that God had put her on that ship, He must also have put the girl there. She spotted the opportunity to develop the heart of a servant – and that meant submitting to the leader who had been placed over her, regardless of how young and apparently unready she might be.

Over the next few months, Lisa did exactly that – and, as she did, an amazing thing happened. The awkward young girl slowly developed into a true leader; with the help of Lisa and others, she saw her gifts flourish and her skill set grow. Before the year was over, she had matured and developed more than anyone had thought possible. Lisa now holds an important leadership position. She knows that she learned how to be a leader, however, by learning first how to become a servant.

Opening up

Read the story above, and then ask the following questions:

- How do you think Lisa felt when she realized that her boss on the ship was an inexperienced eighteen-year-old?

- How do you think you might have reacted if you had been in her place?

- Do you think Lisa made the right decision, or should she have taken charge?

Digging deeper

- How easy or difficult do you find it to submit to those in authority? To teachers? Parents? Youth workers?!

- Try to think of a situation where you chose not to submit, but to argue or rebel. What happened as a result? Do you stand by what you did?

- Now think of a situation in which you chose to back down, and it was hard to do so. Are you glad you submitted in hindsight?

Taking it to the word

Read Ephesians 5:1–2 and 21

- This famous (and controversial) passage in Ephesians tells Christians to live lives submitted to one another – the picture is of everyone submitting themselves to everyone else. What might this look like in practice

  - *In your circle of friends*

  - *In your school*

  - *In your family*

  - *In your church?*

- Agree together some practical ways this week that you will try to "live a life of love", submitting yourself to everyone and becoming "last" (see Jesus' words in Mark 9:35).

The adaptable meeting guide

Meeting aim: To introduce the concept of submission – not as bowing down to authority, but as following Jesus' call to make ourselves "the very last"; to explore seven directions in which we should look to submit ourselves.

Before you start: You will need a number of warm bowls of water, sponges/flannels, towels, and, if you really want to push the boat out, pampering lotions, etc. for the opening activity; relaxing music (optional); seven sheets of paper, each bearing the name of one of the "acts of submission"; a video camera if you are filming the dramas.

Feet!
(10 minutes)

Set up a number of washing-up-bowl-sized containers of warm water. As your group arrives at the venue, the leaders should offer them a foot spa! Some may be reluctant, but try to encourage as many as possible to remove their shoes and socks, and place their feet in a bowl. Do a good job of cleaning their feet – pamper them as much as possible, and try not to let it turn into a joke. Playing some health-spa-style muzak may help to set the scene.

Once a young person has dried their feet, invite them to step into the leader's place and now become the foot-washer. As the activity continues (and when you are no longer among the foot-washers), read out John 13:1–14 (Jesus washes the disciples' feet). Explain that, even though He was their God, Jesus humbled

Himself and washed their feet. And, however badly cared-for or smelly some of the feet in this room are, they would be nothing compared to the dusty, filthy, crusty feet of the disciples. This is one of the great images of Jesus as a servant – He came not to be served, but to serve. Even though He is their king, He submits Himself to them.

Not only that, though – He asks them in verse 14 to respond by washing one another's feet too. This is the activity that the group is now involved in. By doing this, we are submitting to one another. Try to make sure that everyone gets an opportunity to wash someone else's feet.

We can't all win
(10 minutes)

Underline the concept of submission by playing another game together. Choose a team game, such as football or basketball, and play a quick snap game, with one twist: there are no teams – everyone is trying to score; everyone is out for themselves. You may have one or two exceptional people who are able to score, but this will more than likely descend into madness quite quickly.

After the dysfunction of the game has been clearly illustrated, explain that this is a picture of what happens when everyone is out for themselves. Team sports are about submitting our need for personal glory for the good of our team-mates. Let's see what happens when we're not out for ourselves. Quickly divide the group into two teams, and play the game again – this time, the first team to score wins.

Bring the group back together. Explain that these first two

activities are helping us to get a feel for this week's Spiritual Discipline: Submission. This is all about following Jesus' example and submitting ourselves to God and one another. Read Mark 9:35. Note that Jesus doesn't just paint a nice picture, but gets specific. If we want to follow Him, we have to become not just last, but *the very last*. This verse is key to understanding the Spiritual Discipline of Submission. Our aim should be to put *everyone* else's needs and desires before our own.

Seven directions
(20–30 minutes)

Explain that you are now going to look at seven "acts" of submission; seven directions in which we can submit ourselves and "become last". Split into seven groups (minimum numbers are pairs, so if you have fewer than fourteen, just split into as many pairs as you can). Give each group a piece of paper with one of the seven directions written on it. These are:

- *To God*

- *To the Bible*

- *To our family*

- *To our neighbours*

- *To the church*

- *To the broken*

- *To the world.*

Ask each group to spend five minutes brainstorming what it might mean for us as Christians to "submit ourselves" in each of these directions. Then, based on the notes they have made, set them the task of coming up with a one-minute mime, drama, or comedy skit, which illustrates the concept of submission – of making ourselves the very last – in the direction they've been given. Give them a good ten to fifteen minutes to create and rehearse this.

What happens next is up to you. You could spend the next few minutes watching each other's creations, or you could send someone round with a video camera to capture the sketches for later viewing. If you choose the latter option, you will probably find that the groups take the performance much more seriously; you could then use the footage as an introduction to worship, either at the end of the session, or on another occasion. The most important thing is to ensure that all the group members hear and understand what each of the seven "acts" of submission are.

Afterwards, make the point (hopefully illustrated by what the groups have performed) that submission is not the negative act of surrender that modern culture makes out. It frees us from the tiring need always to be right; always to have our own way. Community just doesn't work if everyone is pursuing their own ends with no consideration for one another. Mutual submission makes relationships work.

Submission scruples (10 minutes)

Split into groups, and explain that, in the final activity, they need to come to decisions together – this may involve a fair amount of submission in itself! Read the statements below (or some of your own) from the front, and give them a minute on each to discuss and come up with an answer. Ask for some answers from some of the groups after each discussion – but not all.

1. Tony and Phil are both builders. They both hate bricklaying; they both love operating the machinery. Both jobs need to be done; how do they submit to each another?

2. Charlotte's boyfriend keeps pressuring her to have sex with him, even though she wants to wait. Should she agree to his request, and therefore submit to him?

3. Mike and Carla work together, but do not get on. In an important meeting with their boss, Carla begins to criticize Mike's ability to do the job. Mike has a stack of dirt on Carla – should he use it?

4. Terry walks past a homeless man on the way home from school. The man looks him in the eye and asks him for some spare change. How can Terry practise the Discipline of Submission at this moment?

Wrap-up
(3 minutes)

Ensure that everyone has a satisfactory working definition of this Discipline – and set them the challenge of putting it into practice in the week ahead. Try to make some time at the beginning of the next session for them to feed back on how they practised submission during the week. Pray to close.

ADAPTING THE MATERIAL

For older groups... You may not need to run the sports activity – an explanation may suffice. You could also shorten the drama activity in order to make room for longer discussions about "submission scruples", which they are likely to enjoy.

For younger groups... The final activity may need more guidance to ensure they really "get" the outworking of the Discipline. If you have enough leaders, place one with each group to facilitate the discussion; if not, you could run this as a whole-group activity, rather than splitting.

For churchgoing young people... Really study that verse from Mark (9:35) to explore: what does it mean to be the *very* last? How does this verse link in with Jesus' words in Luke 9:23?

For unchurched young people... There may be a reluctance to get involved in the foot-washing activity. If you think this might be a problem, replace it with something less intrusive – for instance making toast and chocolate spread for one another.

Going deeper: Follow-on activities

1. SUBMISSION IMPOSSIBLE

Get your young people to identify the person, institution or authority that they find it most difficult to submit to. In groups, ask them to explain to each other who or what this is, and why they find it so difficult. Now, in five minutes of quiet, give them each the opportunity to write a letter to that person/group, explaining the issues that they have with them. This could potentially bring some very strong feelings to the surface, so make sure you handle it appropriately.

Create a sanctuary area in your venue, perhaps with a large cross at the centre if you can find one, beanbags, candles or mood lighting, and Bibles. Print out Mark 9:35 and Luke 9:23 on large cards and display them. You could attach these to the cross. Play reflective music in this area. Invite the group members, once they have finished their letters, to bring them to this place, and to read the letters back in the context of the cross.

Jesus performed the ultimate act of submission when He – who was fully God – died at human hands. Though we find these authorities so difficult to submit to, we must learn to follow Jesus' example – and He truly went to extremes. After they have read the letters, trying to find some empathy for the people with whom they struggle, suggest that they remain in this place of sanctuary a little longer, to ask God for His help in living out the Discipline of Submission in every area of their lives, and to listen to Him.

2. LOVING MUM AND DAD

One of the most practical applications of this Discipline for young people is in their relationships with their parents. Obviously, in many cases, family relationships can be complicated, but that shouldn't dissuade you from running this activity.

Hold an evening meal event – possibly at a dressed-up version of your usual meeting venue, or elsewhere – for the parents of the group. Give responsibility for the planning and delivery of the event over entirely to the young people themselves, and make sure that they are involved fully in every step, from preparation to table-waiting and cleaning up. This takes the idea of "honour your father and mother" out of a reactive context, and makes it proactive. By waiting on their parents, the young people are reversing their usual roles. They are used to being served by their parents; this activity is a helpful reminder that God requires them to submit to them.

Week Eight

Give: The Discipline of Service

"By this all men will know that you are my disciples, if you love one another."

John 13:35

I am prone to making a terrible mistake quite often: the mistake of believing that all the good things I see around me come from Christians. That's quite different from believing that all good things come from God – which ultimately they do: instead, it means that when someone commits an act of grace, my immediate question is "I wonder if she's a Christian?"

The practice of Random Acts of Kindness has become popular in Christian circles. Inspired by the 2000 movie *Pay it Forward*, the idea is that you perform loving, encouraging or generous acts for strangers, in the hope that they will "pass on" the love to others. Christians have latched on to the idea as a way both of serving God among their communities, and promoting the values of the kingdom. But it is not only Christians who think this is a good idea. Various groups who have no faith basis, such as the London-based Kindness Offensive, have taken up the same approach because they hope to improve and (though they wouldn't use this word) bless the community around them, and so make the world a better place, albeit on more humanist terms.

So the idea of service is not a uniquely Christian one. What is unique, however, is the Spiritual Discipline of Service.

Self-service

Like many people of my generation, I am a long-standing fan of the American sitcom *Friends*. In one memorable episode ("The One Where Phoebe Hates PBS"), cynic Joey tells his kooky friend Phoebe that there is "no such thing as a selfless good deed". Phoebe sets out to prove him wrong, but in each case Joey proves that, in fact, there is some form of congratulation or reward involved for her. Eventually she thinks she has beaten him as she proudly proclaims: "I let a bee sting me!" She is crushed when Joey reveals the awful news that again prevents this from being a "selfless good deed", explaining that the bee has probably died as a result.

When we choose to serve others, even out of a sense of Christian obedience, we can sometimes have quite mixed motives. We all enjoy the sense of encouragement we feel when we receive thanks; even if we don't realize it, that sensation can subtly become our key motivator for doing further good. Service becomes attractive to us because we know we will be positively affirmed for it, either by those we serve or by those who see us serving. Such affirmation is not bad in itself, but it shouldn't become part of our reason for serving, or indeed for encouraging our young people to serve. The phrase "a thankless task" is always used to describe something negatively – as Christians, we should see such tasks in far more neutral terms, because our service for others is an act of worship. Christian service is selfless, not self-righteous.

Jesus' words on giving are helpful and applicable when we think about service, because serving others is one of the principal ways in which we can give and show generosity.

"When you give to the needy, do not let your left hand know what your right hand is doing, so that your giving may be in secret," He says in Matthew 6:3–4. Of course it is sometimes impossible to serve others without them noticing and offering their thanks, but these verses seem to illustrate that our heart attitude here should be one of submission and humility – we serve selflessly, seeking no earthly reward.

Not word and deed

In recent years, there has been a move within youth evangelism towards marrying proclamation with acts of service. The idea is that word and deed are inseparable when we are trying to demonstrate the love of God to others; that we must both tell people about Jesus, and physically show them the difference He makes. While on one level I applaud this notion, this method of sharing the gospel is not an accurate outworking of the Spiritual Discipline of Service. That isn't a criticism in any way of word and deed mission – it's simply a case of making a distinction.

First, this kind of service is strategic; it often takes place as part of a co-ordinated project or event. It is backed by resources; it is led by para-church agencies, charitable organizations or local church leaders. It is thought-through and targeted; the most "needy" people in an area are identified and then served. None of this is bad; none of this undermines the fact that this is a great response to Jesus' command to love one another; a fine way of following His example, explained in Mark 10:45 when He says that "even the Son of Man did not come to be served, but to serve".

Second, this kind of service is not free of an agenda. When we serve people as part of an evangelistic mission, we are not simply serving them because we love them; we are serving them because we want them to come to know Jesus. We hope that through seeing us giving our time and energy to them for nothing, they will be prompted by the Holy Spirit to ask, "I wonder what motivates them?" This is a wise way of sharing the Good News of Jesus; it demonstrates the love of God and His concern for the poor far better than any tract could. But it is not service for service's sake. As *Friends'* Joey Tribbiani would quickly point out, sharing the gospel like this does not constitute a selfless good deed. Now, you might argue that it is out of our deep love and concern for people that we share the gospel in the first place, and that the greatest way in which we can serve people is by telling them about Jesus. I wouldn't argue with you. My point is simply that the Spiritual Discipline of Service does not work like this.

Service as a response
to God

So what *is* the Discipline of Service? Simply put, it is the natural progression of the Discipline of Submission. As we submit ourselves to God and to others, as we make ourselves "the *very* last", our relationship with all becomes one of service. As we get closer to the heart of God, as our relationship with Him becomes more tangible and real, we cannot help ourselves: we have to serve others. It is an intentional heart attitude, but it is not about thinking strategically. We serve because that is what we are as followers of Christ: servants led by a servant king.

There are, as I understand it, two Greek words that describe time in the New Testament. One, *Chronos*, is the linear, sequential understanding of the word that we use every day. The other, *Kairos*, is more interesting, and seems to more accurately reflect the way Jesus spent His time on earth. Kairos is a description of momentary, perhaps unexpected, chapters of time in which something special happens. The two words are used like this in the Bible – one quantitative, the other qualitative – with Kairos referring to "the appointed time in the purpose of God" (as in Mark 1:15 – "the time has come"). When Jesus encountered people on the road, seemingly at random, He shared Kairos moments with them; tiny chapters of time which turned their lives upside down in an instant.

Practising the Spiritual Disciplines during our everyday Chronos time prepares us for the unexpected and unheralded Kairos moments, when they arrive. They are moments in which we act and speak simply out of the overflow of our relationship with God. If we are living the submitted life, practised in silent listening, rooted in that continual attitude of prayer, then the Kairos moments that arrive will bring with them a certain prompting within. As we encounter others who need an encounter with the love of God, we are led to a point of decision – will we enter into this holy moment and serve the person standing before us, or not? If we respond, an act of service can then take a thousand different forms, and will almost certainly involve an element of self-sacrifice (even sitting to listen to someone who needs to talk involves that). Though it might require the simplest effort from us, an act of service in a Kairos moment can have a profound effect on the people involved.

Of course, in such moments, there is a high probability that God will reveal Himself to those whom we serve; there is a good chance we will be asked to give an account of our motivation for serving and to explain our faith. This is exciting, but, again, not the reason for entering into these moments of service. We serve simply because we must.

Give: Resources

First steps – The discussion starter

CALLED TO SERVE

Jackie Pullinger believed that God Himself had called her to one of the most dangerous parts of the world, to work with people whom no one else wanted to touch. Trying to be obedient to what she believed was God's voice, she left her home in England in 1966 and moved to Hong Kong's notorious Walled City, where she aimed to work as a missionary among the drug addicts and prostitutes who lived there. Despite being in constant danger, she would spend each day trying to build relationships with the people who lived in the slum, hoping to tell them that there was a God who loved them.

Six months into her time in Hong Kong, Jackie was in total despair. She had seen people living in unimaginably bad conditions, yet they didn't want to hear her message of hope. She had achieved almost nothing. Jackie could not work out what she was doing wrong. It simply made no sense to her – after all, if anyone needed a Saviour, it was these people.

Then, after much soul searching, the penny dropped. She had been great at *telling* these people about Jesus – that He loved them and wanted to forgive them – but what she hadn't done was *show* them. Her message consisted entirely of words, in a place where actions spoke far louder. She didn't need just to tell them about Jesus; she needed to *be* Him to them.

From that moment, Jackie radically altered her approach. She spent her time providing food and shelter for those who had none, visiting prisons and becoming an advocate for people with no voice. Instead of words, these practical acts of service soon became the thing she was known for. And before long she was having a profound impact on the city.

Jackie set up a church and a charity within the city and, through the work of both, countless individuals have been completely changed. Lives that seemed hopeless have been turned around, and in every sense saved.

Although the Walled City has long since been demolished, the church still stands, and her organization – the St Stephen's Society – has an impact on people all over the world. The focus has never changed for Jackie, however; all these years later she still shares the love of God with people, through serving them.

Opening up

Read the story above, and then ask the following questions:

- What do you think went through Jackie Pullinger's mind after six fruitless months in a slum? How do you think she felt about God?

- Why was her change in approach so successful?

- Why do you think Jackie chose to do all this?

- What is the difference between telling someone about God's love, and showing them?

Digging deeper

- How do you feel about the idea of serving other people without any reward?

- What are some examples of situations in which you have seen others serve you? What motivated them?

Taking it to the word

Read John 13:31–35

- Why does Jesus say that the way people will know His disciples is by the way they love one another? What will this show them?

- What would it mean for you to love others in the way that Jesus means here?

- How does following Jesus compel people to serve one another?

- What is one practical way in which you could serve someone purely out of love this week – without looking for any reward?

The adaptable meeting guide

Meeting aim: To explore Service as a Spiritual Discipline, as the natural progression from submission, and as a natural response to God.

Before you start: Obtain any relevant parental consent for the "service field trip" – preferably well in advance of the session. Make sure you understand the distinction between *Chronos* and *Kairos* time for the closing epilogue.

Prayer and recap
(10 minutes)

Recap on the previous session, where we looked at the Discipline of Submission. Make sure you remind the group of Jesus' call to us to be the *very* last: to love and submit to one another, to the world, and to God. If you used a video camera in the previous session to record the "acts of submission" dramas, you could play these back to the group now as a reminder.

Explain that, today, you are going to get your hands dirty by diving into the very practical Discipline of Service – an activity of the Christian life that follows closely on from submission. If submission is about changing our heart and attitudes, then service is about putting those ideas into action. In a few moments, you are going to head out on to the local streets to "serve".

Before you do, however, spend a few minutes in prayer together, asking God to create opportunities for service, to bring people across your path who need help, and for wisdom, safety and protection.

Service field trip
(30 minutes – 3 hours)

You are now going to leave the safety of your normal venue and encounter the "world" in order to serve it in the name of Jesus. This can work in a number of ways: I have listed three ideas below, but feel free to create your own service experiment, one which will perfectly fit your context and the young people you are working with. Whatever you decide, here are a few guiding principles:

- **Safety first** – *make sure you have an increased number of adult leaders / helpers / parents on the trip. Ensure that you have carried out a thorough risk assessment in advance, in line with your church / organization's policies. It may also be wise not to* *broadcast your intended location for the activity in advance via social networking sites, etc. In short – take whatever steps you feel you need to in order to be able to relax and feel safe during the trip.*

- **Expect the unexpected** – *before the activity you will be asking God to move; so don't be surprised when He does. That means being a little relaxed about how long things might take, or how much or how little might be "achieved". If our aim is truly to serve, then we need to be open both to where the Spirit is leading and to the genuine needs that people have (rather than those we perceive them to have).*

- **Listen** – *let's be careful not to tell people what kind of help they are looking for, but to listen and respond to what they are actually saying.*

• **Be brave** – *encourage your young people, and your leaders and other adults, to be bold in offering help, and in explaining (when asked) who you are, and why you are doing this. But…*

• **Don't ram the gospel down people's throats** – *this activity is not about covert evangelism; it is about our natural physical response to the spiritual call to serve others. So, if you are asked about your faith or your motivation, of course you should talk about it; just don't try to force or manufacture that. Loving our communities as an act of obedience to God is an end in itself.*

Field trip 1: Find out in advance about a specific need in your community: perhaps there is an elderly couple near you who don't have the ability or resources to keep their garden tidy; a wall of graffiti that the local council is doing nothing about – and address it together. Make sure you have the right tools for the job, and roll your sleeves up together. No one gets to sit on the sidelines; everyone has to get involved. If you have a particularly large or small group, make sure the size of the activity isn't either overwhelming or too easy. If it's a large group, for instance, you might take on several gardens in the same street.

Field trip 2: Hand out free stuff. Adapt this to your context, the time of year, and the specific needs of your community. You could hand out bottles of water in a city centre on a hot summer's day, Easter eggs at Easter, or small gifts at Christmas. I know of a group that regularly knocks on the doors of all the homes on a nearby council estate and hands out gifts – once it was a mug; another time a small clock. The residents treasure these gifts, because they were given with no strings attached.

As an extension of this, you could use these face-to-face encounters to ask local people: what could we do for you? Do they have a pile of rubbish that needs clearing; a shed with a leaking roof; an overgrown front garden? Do they need respite from the responsibilities of caring for someone? If you want to take service really seriously as a group, you could "collect" local needs in this way, and then try as a group (and perhaps as a wider church) to meet them. Again, you should exercise care – both with regard to personal safety and in managing the expectations of the people to whom you are offering help. It's always best to under-promise and over-deliver, rather than the other way around.

Field trip 3: Visit a residential home for the elderly (arranged in advance). Ask the young people in pairs (minimum) to sit and listen to the residents. Many of them will not have people to talk to for much of the day, and even though they may not always make sense, they will be immensely blessed by having someone sit and simply listen to them. Get others to help the carers – who are often poorly paid and work long hours – in whatever ways they need. This might mean peeling potatoes in the kitchen, answering the phone for an hour, or simply making them a cup of tea and listening to them.

Debrief
(10–20 minutes)

Depending on how long you spent on the "field trip", either close the session with a debrief and another look at service, or build this into the start of your next session. With the group all together, share stories of what happened. Ask: how did you feel? Was it exciting / rewarding / scary? Do you feel you made a difference?

Split into groups, and get them to look at John 13:31–35, and discuss the following:

- How does the activity you've just been involved in respond to Jesus' message here?

- If Jesus has left (ready to return at another time), how can we step into the gap and "be" Him to the world around us?

- What does Jesus mean when He says that the way people will know His disciples is by the way they love one another?

- What would it mean for you to love others in the way that Jesus means here?

Epilogue: Kairos and Chronos (5 minutes)

Bring the group back together for a final thought. Explain the difference between *Chronos* time (linear time as we experience it every day) and *Kairos* time (specific moments that arrive, perhaps unexpectedly, and contain opportunities given by God to change lives). See the introduction to the section for more on this. Encourage your young people: the Discipline of Service is about being prepared for those Kairos moments, recognizing them, and then discovering the opportunity to respond to need as it arises. This might mean stopping to buy a coffee for a homeless person, or cancelling your plans to go and spend time with a hurting friend. Brainstorm some more applications of this and then challenge your group: are their eyes, ears and spiritual sensors open for these opportunities to serve God in the week ahead? Pray to close, and make sure you make time at the start of the next session to share any stories that emerge in the next week.

ADAPTING THE MATERIAL

For older groups... Encourage the spirit of social entrepreneurship off the back of this session. If some of the young people feel inspired to start a new initiative, perhaps reaching out to the sorts of people you met in the field-trip activity, then get behind them. Help them to formulate and refine their ideas, and support them as they take ideas for service projects forward – perhaps looking for buy-in from the adult church (if relevant).

For younger groups... You may want to gravitate towards "field trip" option 2 – this is a good first step in serving others, meeting them on neutral territory and handing them a simple token of our care for them.

For churchgoing young people... This is a great opportunity to get outside the church building and into the local community. Don't allow this to turn into a proclamation-motivated outreach; that is totally valid, but today you are simply living out the Discipline of Service – responding to practical needs with practical love.

For unchurched young people... This is a brilliant activity for those who don't yet know Jesus – a great way to demonstrate to them that being a Christian is about making a positive change in the world. We can definitely honour and serve the purposes of God before we commit to a relationship with Him, so use the discussion time afterwards to explore the servant nature of Jesus, and how serving others simply makes sense in practice.

Going deeper: Follow-on activities

1. TREASURE HUNT

An opportunity to be prophetic, to ask God to create Kairos opportunities, and to give young people the chance to see them being created. Gather together with your group for a half-hour prayer meeting before heading out into your local community. This may be a little out of their comfort zone – and yours – but ask God to speak to you during this time; to give you words or pictures that provide specific information which you can follow during the subsequent time of service. Listen to God during this time, and record everything that anyone thinks *might* be a word from Him. Examples of "information" might be: a description of an item of clothing; a place where someone will be; a name; a specific need (for much more on this, see the book *The Ultimate Treasure Hunt* by Kevin Dedmon, Destiny Image Books, 2007).

Armed with information, head out in teams to the local community, and start looking for the people whom God might be drawing to your attention. Be prepared to be bold and – in a worldly sense – make fools of yourselves. Approach people as you feel led, always being open about who you are and what you are doing. Ask specifically – is there a way that we can serve you? This might be through prayer, or through booking an appointment to go and clear their back garden together at a later date. By no means shy away from the gospel message in this, but remember also that it is primarily about fulfilling our commitment to "love one another" through counter-cultural service.

2. RANDOM ACTS OF KINDNESS

Launch a kindness offensive on your local community. Give the group a small budget, and encourage them to dream big about how they can use this money, some of their own, and other resources to bless people in their community. Get them to brainstorm inventive ways of serving people at random – demonstrating that the unconditional love of Jesus is for anyone and everyone.

Then spend an afternoon/evening together in the heart of the community, looking for every opportunity to spring a surprise blessing. Random Acts of Kindness might include:

- *Paying the bus fare / coffee bill / other expense of the person behind you in the queue*

- *Helping a park-keeper or road-sweeper to pick up litter*

- *Loading a parking meter as someone drives up to it*

- *Taking some home-baked biscuits to the local police station or other local service*

- *Smiling at people!*

Part Three: TOGETHER

The Corporate Disciplines

Week Nine

Choose: The Discipline of Worship

What is worship? Is it the words that we sing, or the way that we sing them? Or is it something bigger than that? Is worship somehow possible in everything we do, in every choice we make? Do we have an opportunity, at every juncture of our day, to perform an act of worship? I believe that we do – and that the practice of the Spiritual Disciplines is one of the key ways in which we can prepare our hearts for those opportunities as they arise. Every decision, big or small, contains within it the chance to sin, or the chance to honour God. Every day, every turning point, we do either a right or a wrong thing. The Discipline of Worship is about choosing the right path, time after time, and in doing so glorifying the God who has changed us.

Worship is the opposite of sin

The resources in this book have been road-tested ahead of publication; in one instance, I was running the activity found in the "Week Zero" meeting guide called "The UnSpiritual Disciplines". I was asking the group to come up with opposites to the Disciplines, and, when we reached worship, someone called out that "the opposite of worship is sin". I had to think about that for a moment, but I soon realized that he was profoundly correct. Worship and sin are polar opposite responses to God. They are the day-by-day processes by which we either accept God or reject Him; run towards His open arms or hike off in our own direction.

It is perhaps obvious, but worship and sin cannot co-exist. We cannot honour God and reject Him at the same time. When King David, that great worshipper from the Old Testament, fell from grace with an adulterous affair that cost his mistress' husband his life, his worship fell silent. His passion for God, which had attracted all Israel to follow him as leader, had become compromised. It was left to the prophet Nathan, to bring him back to the right path, to show him what a complete idiot he had been.

In 2 Samuel 12, Nathan not only rebukes David, but delivers some terrible news: as a result of David's sin, his young son will now die. Realizing his utter foolishness, David pleads with God that this won't happen – he prays and fasts in the hope that God might change him mind. He doesn't, and the boy dies. What David does next is telling: even though he must have been filled with grief and anger, both at his own actions and at God, he cleans himself up, changes his clothes... and *worships* God. This is the way in which the Bible shows us that David has fully turned from his sin. In spite of the terrible cost he has paid, he chooses to worship. He has moved from one end of the scale to the other.

Worship is a choice

David made a choice. Each day, we make choices too. This is at the very heart of the Spiritual Discipline of Worship. In his famous song "Blessed be your name", Matt Redman wrote about his heart "choosing" to worship. Worship isn't just something we do; it's something we decide to do.

Richard Foster calls worship "the human response to the divine initiative". God draws us to Himself; He is constantly calling us to worship Him, and that is what He created us for. That doesn't make Him an egotist – it simply means that He knows what is best for us, and that is a life which honours Him and follows His direction. So in every moment God gives us an opportunity to respond in a way that is right and which brings Him glory.

The decision on *how* we respond, however, rests with us. How does this look in practice? It is visible in a hundred thousand tiny moments of our lives. Do we hold the door open for the woman with the pushchair, or make out that we haven't seen her? Do we give away the note in our wallet and forsake the coffee and doughnut we've been pining for, or keep it and donate our loose change instead? Do we take the best seat in the cinema row, or leave it for the person shuffling along behind us? Rooted in our continual attitude of prayer, and drawing on the other Disciplines as we journey through each day, our lives are full of a multitude of opportunities to practise the Discipline of Worship; this Discipline of choice.

Fully engaging in a formal "act of worship" requires a choice too. Worship is never passive, or, rather, it shouldn't be. Standing in a church, simply reading the words on the screen or in the hymn book with an entirely disengaged brain, does not constitute worship. Worship comes from the heart, not the mouth. So when we address God through an act of worship, we should care about what we're saying, singing or doing. It should be as focused and targeted as a prayer; since it is aimed at someone, it should not be aimless.

I have stood in churches with a few faithful young people who desperately want to be part of the adult congregation but find precious little there aimed at them. They sing old hymns that haven't been explained to them; they struggle through lengthy times of often-prosaic prayer. I am amazed by them, because their presence alone demonstrates their heart attitudes – they want to worship God. They have chosen to draw close to Him, instead of taking the much warmer, easier and more fun-filled paths on offer.

I have also stood in church and felt totally disconnected from God. Of course, this is entirely my perception, but we've probably all had those times. The music, the prayers, the sermon – even the "fellowship" time with other Christians – feel utterly barren, bereft of any divine energy. In those times, we again have a choice – and here it seems all the more difficult *and* important – to worship. We can force ourselves to sing the words and mean them; we can concentrate with all our might as others pray. We can take notes in the sermon in the knowledge that tomorrow we may be better placed to reflect on the message. These are not the actions of a fraudulent Christian, but of a mature one.

Together and alone

The Discipline of Worship is the first of our two "corporate" Disciplines, so-called because they can be practised in community. However, worship is also in part an outward-facing individual practice, with regard to both the kinds of lifestyle choice already described, and personal acts of worship. Our prayer and devotional lives, for instance, should include both words and actions that reflect a heart of worship.

It clearly isn't an ancient practice, but listening to worship music, either at home or on the move, can involve the practice of the Discipline of Worship. If we simply allow the music to wash over us, just as we might any pop tune, then we are not engaging in worship – even singing along does not necessarily constitute that. However, we can listen intentionally; we can sing along in heartfelt praise. If we think through the words we are hearing, and all the way through we are responding with a silent "Amen", then this is as much an act of worship as sitting in the front row of a church, belting out the songs with our arms raised aloft. In some cases, more so.

Giving, which is an integral part of our worship, is also an activity to be engaged in alone. As referenced in the previous chapter, Matthew 6:3–4 includes Jesus' command that we "give in secret". To intentionally be generous in full view of others is to enjoy our reward now, rather than in heaven. We give as an act of worship to God – and it is between Him and us.

Worship is also a corporate Discipline – one we practise together as communities that follow Jesus. As Christians we are not just called by God as people but as *a* people; we respond to that call together as well as individually. Worship is one of the primary ways in which we can make that "together" response.

When we worship God together, we do so through acts of worship, both formal and informal. Like the Israelites, we sing psalms or hymns; like David in 2 Samuel 6:14, we should be unashamed to literally dance for joy in public!

Most importantly, we join together to share the meal of Holy Communion – in whatever form our church tradition dictates – reflecting Jesus' command for us to do so. As we share the bread and wine (or substitute thereof), we enter into a holy moment together: joined as a body of believers, connected at the same time to the same extraordinary God. Choosing and agreeing to do these things together, with our hearts and souls invested in every moment, is the corporate outworking of the Discipline of Worship.

Worship is a lifestyle

Persuading young people to join together in a few songs isn't, in my experience, all that difficult. Encouraging them to really think about and mean the words they sing is a natural next step, and is also comparably straightforward. What is much more difficult, however, is persuading anyone – young or old – to take that attitude of worship out of the context of corporate worship, and into the challenging, fast-paced, conflict-ridden world of everyday life. Truly practised, the Discipline of Worship is about making simple daily life choices that reflect the same passion for God that we might show in the middle of a "Big Top" festival experience.

This is hard work for the youth leader. It is about making the same simple point a thousand different times, and in as many different ways. The point is this: worship is not about what we do on a Sunday; worship is the way we live our lives. It is an attitude, a lifestyle; a constant series of decisions that move us another step in God's direction, rather than away from Him. What does that mean in practice? Again, this is a matter between each of us and God. All we can do is look to shape that attitude; one which obliterates the heresy of the sacred/secular division, and sees in every situation an opportunity to respond to the beckoning voice of God.

Choose: Resources

First steps – The discussion starter

HERO WORSHIP

Maureen Collins is utterly devoted. Not to a husband, not to children – for she has had no time in her life for either. Nor is she committed to a job; so all-encompassing is her one passion that she has no time for employment. Because Maureen is absolutely, single-mindedly, obsessed with the American singer Barry Manilow.

Maureen's humble home in Birmingham, England is a shrine to her first love; the walls are covered with posters documenting the many decades of Manilow's success. She refuses to listen to the music of any other recording artist, meaning the soundtrack to her life is a repetitive cycle of "Could It Be Magic" and "Copacabana". She has seen her hero perform live all over the world, and although she is by her own admission far too shy to try to speak to him, she has written him hundreds of letters, detailing her great devotion to the man and his music.

Maureen has literally dedicated her life to supporting Manilow's career, cheering his success and creating huge scrapbooks detailing his every media mention. According to a local newspaper interview, she spends most of her days calling radio stations around the United Kingdom, requesting Manilow's songs. Her friends and family have long given up trying to persuade her to tone down her passion.

"From the first time I heard him sing, I knew I never wanted the music to stop," Maureen explains. "He has the power to make me feel like he's singing those songs just to me. That's why I follow him all over the world – I'd go anywhere for Barry."

Opening up

Read the story above, and then ask the following questions:

- Do you think Maureen has wasted her life? Or in some ways has she lived it to the full?

- Why does Maureen continue to follow Barry Manilow so obsessively?

- In what ways does Maureen's support of Barry resemble religious worship?

Digging deeper

- Who are your heroes? What is it about them that you admire?

- How do you show commitment or allegiance to your favourite bands, sports teams or celebrities?

- Does your support of the people you follow or support ever get out of hand?

- Who do you find it easier to get excited and passionate about – these famous heroes, or God?

Taking it to the word

Read John 4:19–26

- Jesus is talking to a woman about various things when the subject of worship comes up. What does Jesus say about it here?

- He seems to be saying that God is actively looking for people who will worship Him. Why do you think He wants that?

- Jesus says (verses 23 and 24) that true worshippers worship in spirit and in truth. What do you think this means?

- What does it mean to worship God? Is it about singing songs, or something else entirely?

The adaptable meeting guide

Meeting aim: To explore not just what worship is, but how it is a Spiritual Discipline, to be both practised alone and entered into together.

Before you start: You will need obstacles for the first activity; flip chart and pens; photocopies of the "worst poem ever written" (you'll find it on the Internet); someone to lead musical worship, and a way of projecting the words; a sheet of A3 paper for each group – and pens; relevant equipment for your "worship stations".

Listen to my voice (5 minutes)

Set up a tricky-to-navigate (but not dangerous) obstacle course in or outside your venue. Blindfold a member of the group, and get them to stand at one end of the course. Now select two members of the group whose voices sound vaguely similar: one will try to navigate the blindfolded person safely through the course; the other one will try to make them crash! Allow the kind voice to introduce itself, and explain to the blindfolded person that they will also hear conflicting voices. Their job is to listen to the right voice – and if they follow those instructions, they'll get through the course safely. Get the game under way – yourself staying close to the blindfolded person to make sure you prevent any possible serious mishaps!

After the game, explain the simple point that our lives are

made up of daily choices about which voice to listen to; which voice to walk towards. Sometimes it might feel very hard, but as Christians we need to try to choose God over the world every time.

What is worship?
(10 minutes)

Get the whole group together, and hold a discussion around a flip chart. Ask them the question: what is worship? Write down everything that comes up – even if you personally disagree. It's likely that your group will focus on "acts of worship" primarily – music, singing, perhaps liturgy and even chanting.

Now read two short sections of the Bible – one an Old Testament reference to sacrifice (Leviticus 1:1–2 and 10–13); the second Paul's rallying call for us to be "living sacrifices" (Romans 12:1–2). Ask: how do these two passages fit together? Explain that they illustrate the difference between God's Old Testament covenant (agreement) with the people through the Law, and His New Testament covenant through Jesus. So what else might worship be? See if they have some more suggestions to add to the flip chart at this point.

By the end of this discussion, make sure that they understand that worship isn't simply about singing; it's about an attitude – a discipline – which extends into every area of our lives, and means making many daily choices: to walk towards God, rather than away from Him.

The worst poem ever written (5 minutes)

Give out copies of the 1880 poem "The Tay Bridge Disaster" by William McGonagall (1825–1902). Explain that this poem is widely regarded as one of the worst ever written. It is a real struggle to read it, but in this activity we're going to discipline ourselves to read all the way to the end. Quietly get them to read the poem.

Afterwards, ask how easy or difficult they found it to get to the end. Explain: if we're honest, sometimes this is how we feel when we come to pray, read the Bible, or worship God. It's a slog; we don't want to be there; we don't *feel* anything. Worship, however, is about making a choice – to be present and to focus ourselves on God, even when we feel totally disconnected and far away from Him.

Sing like you mean it (10 minutes)

Bring in your musical worship leader and ask them to set up. Ask: when you sing in church, how much do you think about the words that are coming out of your mouth? Do you think about them at all – or could you be singing anything? With the previous activity in mind, ask them to join you in singing one or two songs of worship together and, as they do so, challenge them to think through the words they are singing. Afterwards, ask them if this was a different experience of worship for them.

Together alone
(10 minutes)

Get into groups and ask: what are some of the different ways in which we can worship God together? Get each group to brainstorm a list of ways on A3 paper: these might include singing; reading "liturgy" together; serving those in need... What else can they come up with?

Now ask them to repeat the activity, but thinking of ways in which we can worship God on our own (and even in secret). What makes this new list? Which from the first list still apply? Make sure they have included giving on this list (see Matthew 6:3–4). Challenge each of them to choose one thing from this list to practise this week.

Worship stations
(15 minutes)

Set up several worship "stations" around your venue (or another space), which allow your young people to try out and experience various approaches. After five minutes, rotate your groups around these stations. Choose at least three from the list below, or add your own (see www.engageworship.org for a host of great ideas):

- Your worship leader from the earlier activity leads sung worship – this is recommended especially if your group don't usually get a chance to do this.

- Lay out various images of Jesus from the worlds of fine art and film. In the middle have large sheets of paper, on which the young people can write their words of response (description, praise, confusion, etc.) to the images.

- Place a large cross (wooden if possible) in a corner of your venue. Provide postcards, and ask the young people to write a few words of worship (however simple) and pin the postcards onto the cross.

- Chant together, using material from the Taizé community (www.taize.fr/en)

- Print some A4 or A3 sheets with "Worship Jesus" written in the middle. Provide art materials for them to decorate this sheet as they want, as an act of worship.

Epilogue: Worship as a lifestyle (5 minutes)

At the end of the session, explain that many – if not all – of the Spiritual Disciplines lead us to worship. Through fasting we honour God with our bodies; through meditation and solitude we honour Him with our time. Service and submission include elements of worship also, as of course does the final Discipline: celebration. So if prayer underpins the Disciplines, worship is their fruit (output, result, product). As we near the end of this series of meetings on the Spiritual Disciplines, we should now be comfortable with the idea that we "pray continually"; by virtue of practising the Disciplines we should also seek to continually worship God.

ADAPTING THE MATERIAL

For older groups... You could have a longer period of sung worship – especially if this is something that they don't get a chance to enjoy very often in their home context.

For younger groups... Instead of brainstorming a list of worship styles and forms, provide a list and ask them to talk about how they feel about each one. Do they enjoy singing? Do they find giving difficult?

For churchgoing young people... You could split the session over two weeks and, in the first week, end by getting them to imagine and suggest possible worship stations for the final activity. In the second week, you could spend some time building these together, and then spend a longer period (perhaps thirty to forty minutes) working your way around the different stations.

For unchurched young people... Focus on choices – this is the key. Discuss: how easy or difficult do they find it to choose right from wrong? Make it clear that God has given us choice and free will; in fact He gives us daily choices. What do they think are some examples of this? Will we choose to turn against Him (sin), or to follow Him and His ways (worship)?

Going deeper: Follow-on activities

1. WORSHIP THROUGH EVERYTHING

Encourage your young people to take an opportunity in the next week to engage in an activity that they enjoy – something which "feeds their soul". So not watching TV or eating junk food – an activity through which they are made to feel more alive. That might be going out with friends; it might be playing a sport, building or creating something – anything that helps them to truly rest and relax. As they do this they should make themselves aware of the God who gives them all good things; who hands out gifts to them; who loves it when they rest in Him.

So they are to engage in this activity – whatever it is – in an attitude of worship. If they are playing football, they should do so in the knowledge that God is here also, that He is in fitness and skill and the excitement of a game. If they are painting, they should celebrate the creativity that they have received from the creator God. Whatever the activity, they should take part with an attitude of prayer, with an awareness of God's involvement in this and every area of their lives, and, most importantly, with a knowledge that they can turn this into an act of worship.

2. VIDEOS TO GOD

Give a group of young people (with a good mix of skills and ages) a video camera, and set them the task of creating a "video letter" to God. Ask them to go and capture footage of everything in their lives and community that they find important or amazing – this could be images of nature in a local park, spliced together with footage of them playing video games! It just needs to authentically reflect the things for which they are thankful, the things that they find important. Now, (perhaps enlisting the help of one of your tech-savvy young people) get them to write and add a commentary track – a prayer of worship, written to God, explaining to Him why these things are important. Afterwards, watch it together and, as long as no sensitive or copyrighted images appear, consider posting it online for others to enjoy.

Week Ten

Party: The Discipline of Celebration

"Rejoice in the Lord always. I will say it again: Rejoice!"

Philippians 4:4

If we're honest, the word "discipline" usually refers to something that requires sacrifice, even pain. That's why so many of us struggle in the area of self-discipline: it requires an act of the will which doesn't necessarily bring comfortable results. When we think of the Spiritual Disciplines, our minds are likely to turn first to prayer, fasting, and solitude. How many of us think immediately of the ancient Discipline of Celebration?

In Scripture, the idea of celebration is everywhere. Key moments take place around a meal or feasting table. Jesus' first miracle was at a wedding, where he ensured that the alcohol kept flowing even when the supplies had apparently run out (be careful how you handle that story with young people!); His final meeting with the disciples before His death took place at suppertime. At that famous meal, He set in motion a tradition of reverent remembrance in order to give billions of people through the centuries a method of celebrating Him. It took place at

Passover – in itself a Jewish celebration of God's faithfulness in leading the Israelites out of Egypt.

As these examples show, celebration can sometimes be wild and unabashed, sometimes reflective and weighted with great meaning. But, in every case, celebration is ultimately about joy. And practising joy is a Spiritual Discipline that is just as valid and important as all the others. As we talk to young people about the tools with which they can develop a deeper relationship with God, we must not only focus on those that seem difficult and worthy. To neglect the Discipline of Celebration is to empty the Christian faith of one of its greatest truths: that we win.

Party people

The Christian calendar helps us with two major dates around which to orientate our celebration: Christmas and Easter. At times the church does this superbly – throwing open its doors to local communities, communicating the story, conveying this sense of unreserved joy. In recent years I have become part of an Anglican church community after many years in "free" churches. While those places did not neglect the opportunity to celebrate these key moments in the year with great creativity, reverence and joy, there is something very special about the way – including both liturgy and local community engagement – that Anglicans celebrate these festivals. On Easter Sunday, I get literal goosebumps as my vicar bellows out the words "Christ is risen", and a crowd double the size of the regular congregation hollers back: "He is risen indeed; Hallelujah!" The sense of joy is palpable; attractive even. For one Sunday we are clearly marked out as people of celebration.

This provides an unfortunate contrast to the way the church is often viewed, both by the media and by many who refuse to set foot inside one of its buildings. Thanks to decades of placard-waving, campaigning and megaphoning (much of which has been rooted in good biblical teaching, but perhaps with a bit of over-emphasis), many non-Christians picture the church as a hive of negativity, so concerned with what they disagree with and stand against that they've forgotten what they stand *for*. The Discipline of Celebration keeps us in balance; it helps us both to stand against what is wrong, and to visibly stand *for* what is right. We are a "resurrection people" (trendy buzz-phrase at time of writing); we celebrate the Resurrection of Jesus not just on Easter Sunday, but on every single day of our life. Communicating to young people the centrality of joy to the Christian life could make the difference between cultivating a faith that provides an oasis in their lives, and a spiritual desert.

Everyday joy

The Discipline is not merely about directly celebrating what God has done through the cross (although all roads do lead back there). We can also find opportunities to celebrate in every area of our lives, and in the lives of others. Because we are a celebration people, our joy should propel us to take on an attitude of celebration.

So we should look for every opportunity to affirm, encourage, and cheer. We can celebrate successes, and great efforts that didn't quite work out. We can make birthdays and rites of passage times that don't simply involve marking a date, but instead recognize the God-created brilliance of the individual. We should never look down on an evening in which we achieve nothing more than "having fun". In doing simply that, we have embodied what it means to be a community of celebration.

Infectious enthusiasm

Celebration is an activity for the church to practise together. It might seem a little low-brow; a less important Discipline than the rest because it's "easier". Yet if we took it as seriously as we take some of the others, what might happen as a result?

For instance: if we were in fact *obsessed* with finding the positive in others, rather than the negative, how attractive might the church become? If we were known as people of constant celebration – and if we look at the words we use in our Sunday services, that is what we claim to be – how many more people might be persuaded to wander through our doors? Everyone knows what the church stands against (thanks to some of our more extreme brothers and sisters, this list is far longer than any you'll find in the Bible). If we were better at communicating that we stand for fun, for living life in all it's fullness (Jesus' words in John 10:10, not mine), and for squeezing the last drop of life out of every moment... that news could start a revolution.

How does the average non-Christian young person in your area view your church? Boring? Probably – unless it's one of those churches that puts pictures of sparkly-toothed young singers on a city-centre billboard, in which case they most likely think it's a cult. Irrelevant? Almost certainly. They see the church as an institution full of rules; they almost certainly do not see grace.

Practising celebration together as communities of Christians helps to reflect grace to those who look on.

I was recently at an inter-church event held in a park in the centre of town. Far from being the stereotypical ecumenical event, where half the people take a Sunday off and the other half sit grumpily in their tribes, this was a vibrant affair. Everyone involved – including the near 1,000-strong congregation – raised their game because, in such a public space, there were hundred of bemused onlookers. Gloriously, the theme and feel of the event was celebration; unsurprisingly, many of those bemused onlookers kept looking on for the whole hour. When we celebrate together, even in the context of a church service, we become magnetic.

Encouraging party people

If we practise the Discipline of Celebration with young people, teaching them to do likewise, we can potentially see three things happen:

First, celebration **cultivates joy**. A commodity that is in short supply in cynical Western culture, joy is a child-like virtue and a fruit of the Holy Spirit (Galatians 5:22). It is so much easier to be negative, and to drag people down with us, yet as young people discover joy, they realize how foolish the world is. This can be seen practically in acts of generosity or encouragement. In a selfish culture, we are sometimes shocked to discover that it actually feels better to give than to receive; that making someone else's day can radically improve our own. When we learn to celebrate one another, and look for the good in every situation, joy is unleashed.

Second, celebration **makes us stronger**. Nehemiah 8:10 says "the joy of the Lord is your strength", and experience tells us it's true. The journey of faith requires perseverance – how much harder we make things for ourselves when we deny joy! Much of this book has been concerned with ensuring that young people are not discipled in such a way that leaves them brittle; the Discipline of Celebration is vital in ensuring that faith isn't lopsided, and therefore substantially weaker than it should be.

Third, **celebration creates community**. This isn't any great revelation: we know from experience that human beings meet and socialize better at a wedding than a funeral. Our challenge is to have more of the characteristics of the former than the latter – and theologically of course this makes perfect sense! What the Discipline perhaps helps us to do here is see the "spiritual" element to those parts of our youth work programme that might seem more peripheral: the bowling nights and the BBQs. When we practise joy together, we cannot fail to be drawn closer together.

In practice

Of all the Disciplines, Celebration is perhaps the least intuitive to explain to young people, simply because we don't always think of it in spiritual terms. We should however be intentional about doing so; it is as vital as all the others. Some practical ideas contained within the resources that follow are designed for them to adopt and use regularly, but more simply even than that, we should look for straightforward ways to remind them of this "forgotten" Discipline. Meditate together on the "joy" aspects of our faith. Build in time at the beginning of each youth session where they each find another person to encourage. Establish set times each year (and term) to celebrate together – what God has done; who he has made, and the communities he has placed us in together.

* * *

Completing the course

If you are running *The Beautiful Disciplines* as a course, you have reached the end. It is a fitting place to finish our journey – a real high note – and so I have suggested that you frame the final session in the context of a party. One of the suggestions in the final meeting guide is that you give your young people another copy of the "God Audit" from Week "Zero", in order to help them to see how their faith has moved on during the course. If you have the luxury of further time, however, you could consider holding an extra session after this one, at which young people can raise any questions they may have as a result of the course, and share stories of what God has done through the various activities and practices.

This short course has hopefully introduced the young people with whom you work to a range of tools through which they can personally connect with God. Like you, I hope that these will strengthen their faith, and help them to develop a relationship with God that lasts. However, they (like you) are desperately human, and, with all the best intentions, may over time begin to relax again their commitment to that relationship. Therefore, if you really want to get the best out of these resources, it might be a good idea to hold refresher sessions every six months or so, which simply recap the Disciplines, allow for stories to be shared, and involve a more informal version of the "God Audit".

I hope and pray that these resources have been helpful, that my rambling introductions have provided some sort of thought-provoking context, and, most importantly of all, that you have seen young lives changed as a result of helping them to draw near to God. These ancient tools have been achieving that for thousands of years; choosing to rediscover them might be one of the most important youth ministry decisions you've ever made.

Party: Resources

First steps – The discussion starter

I WISH IT COULD BE CHRISTMAS EVERY DAY...

Christmas comes but once a year... unless, that is, you happen to live with Wiltshire electrician Andy Park, a man who loves the festive period so much he's even rechristened himself "Mr Christmas".

Since July 1993, Mr Park has celebrated Christmas every single day. He claims to get through hundreds of turkeys, crackers, and bottles of sherry each year, as he goes through his unusual daily routine. He begins each day with a breakfast of leftovers and mince pies before going to work, returning each afternoon for a full turkey dinner, which he eats while watching a recording of the Queen's speech. Afterwards, he unwinds with a classic Christmas Day film, and falls asleep on the sofa. He has a permanent Christmas tree erected in his living room, and claims to have gone through over thirty artificial trees, 10,000 balloons and 10 km of tinsel in an effort to keep his decorations fresh.

In 2005, Mr Park released an inevitable Christmas single, called "It's Christmas every day". Perhaps unsurprisingly, it failed to mount a serious challenge for the festive Number One spot. Since then, things have begun to look a little more bleak for Mr Christmas. He admitted in 2007 that the economic recession was forcing him to scale back his daily celebrations, and around the same time his doctor warned him that his stuffing-heavy lifestyle – which had seen him grow to nineteen stone in weight – was beginning to have a dangerous impact on his health.

Regardless of all this party-pooping, Mr Park continues to celebrate each day (although he is rumoured to take a day off on Christmas Day itself).

"I'll never forget the day it started," he explains. 'The sun was shining, but I was just feeling fed up and bored, so I went home and put the decorations up. Suddenly I was happy. I thought, this is fun. So I did it again the next day, and the day after that."

Opening up

Read the story above, and then ask the following questions:

- Why do you think Andy Park continues to celebrate Christmas every day?

- What is it that makes Christmas so much fun and so enjoyable – for some people at least?

- Do you imagine Mr Park to be a lonely person, or surrounded by friends and acquaintances? Why?

- Would you want to go for Christmas dinner with Mr Christmas?

Digging deeper

- How much of your time do you spend partying and celebrating? Is it too much time, too little, or just right?

- Do you think there's a spiritual side to party and celebration?

Taking it to the word

Read Psalm 150:1–6

- What is the mood of this psalm? Do you see Christians today getting this excited about God?

- Why is following God a cause for excitement and celebration?

- Is the church best known for celebrating? How might things change if that was how the church was known?

The adaptable meeting guide

Meeting aim: To teach young people that celebration and joy are central to our faith; to explore how we are a "celebration people"; to look at how Celebration is a Spiritual Discipline in itself, and how we can practise it together.

Before you start: Either this meeting could take place in a completely different venue from the one in which you normally meet, or you could go all-out in redecorating your normal venue. Either way, you are decking out your meeting space as a place to PARTY! Since most teenage parties include elements that probably aren't appropriate in a youth-work context(!), you're going to set out the room as if you're holding a children's birthday party. Supermarkets do cheap decorations, hats, tablecloths, serviettes, etc., and staple food like jelly and ice cream are available quite cheaply.

You will also need: party bags to give away at the end; cheap party favours, sweets, etc. with which to fill the bags, enough cake for everyone; party music; shoe box and paper slips for the "celebrating each other" activity; parcel(s) wrapped with sweets and Bible verses in every layer; two buckets of water and pairs of various fruits, vegetables and objects for the extreme bobbing; towels; "Gasp", "Boo", "Cheer" and "Applause" A4 cards for holding up; copies of the God Audit (optional, see Appendix i).

Turn up, tune in, chill out (10 minutes plus)

Have the young people arrive to find a party atmosphere. Do whatever you can with regard to music, lighting and decoration to communicate that a) this is a very different session from what they might normally expect, and b) this is going to be all about celebration and having fun. Encourage them to relax, and for the first few minutes enjoy a bit of party food and some time to chat together.

Pass thy parcel
(10 minutes)

Play your first fun game with a twist – a game of pass the parcel which also celebrates the promises of God. This obviously needs to have been planned well in advance: pass round a circle a parcel, wrapped in enough layers for everyone in the group to get a chance to tear one off. In between each layer you should place two things: a small sweet or fun-size chocolate bar, and a Bible verse (written in full, not a reference). As your group pass the parcel (stopping each time the music stops), get those who win each round to read out their Bible verse to the group before you restart.

Some ideas for great verses that you might want to use: Genesis 28:15; Psalm 27:1–2; Psalm 66:9; Matthew 28:18; Luke 24:34; 2 Corinthians 2:14; 2 Thessalonians 3:3.

Celebrating each other
(5 minutes)

Explain that you also want to celebrate the uniqueness of one another, so set up an "encouragement box" – a shoebox with a hole cut out of it – and ask everyone to take some time to write down at least one message for one other member of the group. These should celebrate, build up, and be honest (you may need to filter some out!) Examples might include:

- *Dave W, you are brilliant because you make everyone laugh.*

- *Sarah, I thought it was really inspiring when you told your story in church at the baptism service; thank you!*

- *Simon, you are a really great listener – thanks for listening to me.*

Ask them not to sign the notes, but to post them anonymously. To make sure that everyone receives at least one message of encouragement, get your team of leaders to prepare at least one for every member of your group – but only refer to these if necessary. Continue to collect these messages during the rest of the session.

After you have explained this, allow a bit more time for the group to simply relax together and enjoy the party, before the next activity begins. This will also give them some time to submit some encouraging messages to the box.

UBC: Ultimate Bobbing Championship (10 minutes)

Split the group into two teams, and gather together for a competition that will test them to their physical limits... well, sort of. Place two buckets of water a short distance apart on each table, and place an apple in each. Ask each team to choose a competitor to take part in an apple-bobbing challenge. Get the two who are chosen to "bob" (grab at them with only their mouths) for the apples, and award a point to the winner. Have towels on standby!

Now ask for another volunteer from each team, and this time, instead of apples, place a different fruit, vegetable or object in each bucket. This could theoretically be anything; the only rules are that the objects are the same, safe, grabbable-by-mouth, and, of course, objects that float (some possibilities: sponges, Brussels sprouts, "fun-size" chocolate bars, rubber ducks, balloons, ice cubes, boiled eggs… but use your imagination!). Now run the activity again… and again, until either they get bored or a clear winner emerges. Award a small prize to the winners. To the victorious team say something along the lines of: "Congratulations, you are a very talented team of ultimate bobbers. As Christians, we want to continually celebrate in one another the various talents God has given us, however small or ridiculous they might seem." Yes, it's tenuous, but the message *is* there… and it'll be a lot of fun! Refer the group again to the encouragement box, which they still have time to add to.

Rowdy resurrection (15 minutes)

Make sure everyone has a (soft) drink, and bring out some cake! Distribute these, and then get everyone to gather round, food and drink in hand, to listen to a story. The atmosphere you're trying to create here is much like that at the speeches at a wedding or birthday party. Explain that you are going to read an account of the resurrection of Jesus. This is a story of victory – about how love has conquered death – it is exciting, compelling, amazing! When we hear it, we should want to cheer… and that's exactly what we're going to do. Have a leader or volunteer stand alongside you with the "Gasp", "Boo", "Applause", and "Cheer" cards at hand. As you get to the relevant parts of the story (indicated below), they hold up the appropriate sign, and the crowd has to follow their instructions. Explaining that the story starts at the moment of Jesus' death, now read the account from Matthew (27:50–52, 54, 57–66: 28:1–10) as dramatically as you can:

> ... When Jesus had cried out again in a loud voice, he
> gave up his spirit. **[GASP]** At that moment the curtain of
> the temple was torn in two from top to bottom. **[GASP]**
> The earth shook, the rocks split and the tombs broke
> open. **[GASP]** The bodies of many holy people who had
> died were raised to life. **[GASP]** When the centurion
> and those with him who were guarding Jesus saw
> the earthquake and all that had happened, they were
> terrified, and exclaimed, "Surely he was the Son of
> God!"**[CHEER]**
>
> As evening approached, there came a rich man from
> Arimathea, named Joseph, who had himself become a
> disciple of Jesus. **[APPLAUSE]** Going to Pilate **[BOO]**, he
> asked for Jesus' body, and Pilate ordered that it be given
> to him. Joseph took the body, wrapped it in a clean linen
> cloth, and placed it in his own new tomb that he had
> cut out of the rock. He rolled a big stone in front of the
> entrance to the tomb and went away. Mary Magdalene
> and the other Mary were sitting there opposite the tomb.
>
> The next day, the one after Preparation Day, the
> chief priests and the Pharisees **[BOO]** went to Pilate.
> **[BOO]** "Sir," they said, "we remember that while he was

still alive that deceiver said, 'After three days I will rise again.' So give the order for the tomb to be made secure until the third day. Otherwise, his disciples may come and steal the body and tell the people that he has been raised from the dead. This last deception will be worse than the first." **[BOO]**

"Take a guard," Pilate answered. "Go, make the tomb as secure as you know how." So they went and made the tomb secure by putting a seal on the stone and posting the guard. **[BOO]**

After the Sabbath, at dawn on the first day of the week, Mary Magdalene and the other Mary went to look at the tomb. There was a violent earthquake, **[GASP]** for an angel of the Lord came down from heaven and, going to the tomb, rolled back the stone and sat on it. **[GASP]** His appearance was like lightning, and his clothes were white as snow. The guards were so afraid of him that they shook and became like dead men. **[CHEER]**

The angel said to the women, "Do not be afraid, for I know that you are looking for Jesus, who was crucified. He is not here; **[CHEER]** he has risen, **[CHEER]** just as he said. Come and see the place where he lay. Then go quickly and tell his disciples: 'He has risen from the dead **[CHEER]** and is going ahead of you into Galilee. There you will *see* him.' **[CHEER]** Now I have told you." **[APPLAUSE]**

So the women hurried away from the tomb, afraid yet filled with joy, and ran to tell his disciples. Suddenly Jesus met them. **[CHEER]** "Greetings," he said. **[CHEER]**

They came to him, clasped his feet and worshipped him.
Then Jesus said to them, "Do not be afraid. Go and tell
my brothers to go to Galilee; there they will see me."
[CHEER + APPLAUSE]

(Based on NIV)

After you've finished the reading, underline the point that this
is a story about victory being snatched from the jaws of defeat.
Jesus wins! Jesus has won! As Christians, we're not crucifixion
people; we're not the people of death. Rather, we're a resurrection
people – we are all about life, and life to the full! This is what we
should be known for – this is how the world should see us. Not
as people who criticize, find fault, and choose to be negative,
but as people who celebrate because they have a reason to be
full of joy!

Celebrating each other
(5 minutes)

Read out a selection of the messages which have been submitted
to the "encouragement box". Ask a few: how does it feel to hear
that kind of message about yourself? Did they enjoy writing them?
Why do they think we're so bad at being encouraging sometimes?
Challenge them not to stop – but to begin to build the practice
of encouragement into all their relationships, remembering how
good it feels not only to give, but also to receive it!

Epilogue: Keep celebrating (5 minutes)

Keep the group together for just a few more minutes, as you explain the importance of the Discipline of Celebration to them. They may feel like this was a really easy session compared to the others – or that they haven't really learned anything this week. Make sure they understand that celebration – the daily practice of joy – is just as important as all the other Disciplines; and that if we're going to attract others to join us, it's one that we need to be known for practising in abundance! Explain that celebration (see the introductory chapter for more on this):

- **Grows our sense of joy** *(Galatians 5:22); helping us to look for the good in every situation, and to be a force of positive change in our communities*

- **Makes us stronger** *(Nehemiah 8:10); helping us to persevere and keep going in the tough times of our lives and the empty periods of our faith, and making us balanced, so we're not only known for being critical of things in the world that aren't right, but also for celebrating what is good*

- **Creates community**, *providing us with opportunities to grow meaningful relationships with others. Friendships don't grow in an atmosphere of negativity, cynicism and criticism, but flourish when we celebrate together and enjoy one another.*

As you finish, encourage everyone again to take this Spiritual Discipline as seriously as they have the other nine. If we practise joy every day, in our schools, families and communities, we reflect to the whole world that the Good News about Jesus, really is good!

Party bags

As everyone leaves the meeting, hand out goodie bags containing cake, sweets, toys, and anything else you can think of. In addition you might want to include a copy of the "God Audit" (see Appendix I) and perhaps also some other useful gifts such as a sample of Bible reading notes.

ADAPTING THE MATERIAL

For older groups... Don't assume they won't want to play children's games – if anything, they'll relish the opportunity to play and have childish fun for a couple of hours! You might even want to increase more games – Simon Says, Musical Statues, balloon races and the like – and allow them to capitalize on this one-off opportunity they have to be children again.

For younger groups... Conversely, those who have only just grown out of these sorts of parties may find the activities a little patronising. Be mindful of this – particularly in the case of "Pass Thy Parcel" – you might want to replace this with a high-energy ball game like dodgeball... just watch out for spillages with all that food and drink around!

For churchgoing young people... *Don't* try to up the "God" content. Really focus on helping them to see that joy is a spiritual commodity.

For unchurched young people... The focus isn't so much on the witness that we give to the outside world, as on experiencing joy together during the meeting. The key aim is to give these young people a truly enjoyable experience within a context that they would understand as "church". To that end, you may even want to hold the party in a church building.

Going deeper: Follow-on activities

1. PARTY PLANNERS

Hypothetically: give your group – or smaller sub-groups – a £150 budget with which to plan their own end-of-year party. Encourage them to be really creative to ensure that the money stretches as far as possible; suggest they also pick a theme for the event. The aim is to plan something that enables them to practise the Discipline of Celebration together; the point is simply to enjoy being alive, and being loved by God!

Later: if the budget allows, take these ideas and put on a real end-of-term event which includes as many of those ideas as possible (if you are running the activity with several groups pick a "winner"). Involve the young people – especially those who came up with the ideas – in planning and putting it on.

2. #LOVEMONDAY

Encouraging each other is a huge part of the Discipline of Celebration, because it helps us to celebrate one another; how we have been made, and the gifts that each of us has been given.

#LoveMonday is an initiative that a few youth workers started on the social networking website Twitter, in early 2011. It is a very simple concept – members of the site choose three people each Monday to whom they will send a simple message of encouragement. Thanks to the site's 140-character limit, Twitter forces us to get straight to the point, and that often means that people say exactly what they mean to each other, because they don't have time to waffle! The idea is that each person who receives one of these messages then "pays forward" the encouragement they have received to three more people, so the message of love, affirmation and encouragement spreads virally through the site each Monday. In the first instance, why not get any of your team and your young people to join in with #LoveMonday each week.

More immediately though, apply the same idea in a physical meeting. Get everyone to stand up, and walk around the room saying something encouraging to each person (minimum three) that they meet. Each could be either a simple word about their personality/character (try to dissuade them from making comments about appearance), or it could be a specific encouragement about something they have said or done in the past. Run the activity for as long as you want – and keep it in mind for the next time you're involved with an adult church.

We're sometimes very bad at encouraging one another, yet just as it feels as good as to receive, encouragement also makes both the speaker and the receiver feel great!

Appendix I

God Audit

For use before and after taking part in the Beautiful Disciplines course

This simple worksheet is designed to help you think about your current relationship with God. As you grow as a Christian, you can answer the questions again and again, and then compare your results over time to chart the progress of your deepening faith.

1. In a sentence, how would you describe your relationship with God, right now?

2. How would you like to see this change in the future (one to two sentences)?

_____

_____

_____

3. Rate the following ten statements from 1–10, "1" meaning "very strongly disagree", "10" meaning "very strongly agree." Circle the number that best reflects your answer.

a) Prayer is a central part of my life

1 2 3 4 5 6 7 8 9 10

b) I am committed to regular Bible study

1 2 3 4 5 6 7 8 9 10

c) Fasting is part of my spiritual life

1 2 3 4 5 6 7 8 9 10

d) I meditate regularly on Scripture, on God, and on my own journey with Him

1 2 3 4 5 6 7 8 9 10

e) I am actively trying to live my life simply

1 2 3 4 5 6 7 8 9 10

f) I am comfortable with silence and practise listening to God

1 2 3 4 5 6 7 8 9 10

g) I am committed to submitting myself to others, and to *always* putting them first

1 2 3 4 5 6 7 8 9 10

h) Serving others is a natural part of my life; I take every opportunity to serve

1 2 3 4 5 6 7 8 9 10

i) I live my life as an act of worship, and turn from sin at every opportunity

1 2 3 4 5 6 7 8 9 10

j) My faith is about joy and celebration; I encourage others and share that joy wherever I can

1 2 3 4 5 6 7 8 9 10

Return to these three questions again soon, and compare your answers each time you do. Where have you moved forward as you seek to become more like Jesus? Where have you perhaps slipped back a bit? What do you need to do to make sure you've moved further along these lines when next you come to evaluate this?

YOUTHWORK MAGAZINE

Martin Saunders is the Editor of *Youthwork* magazine, the UK's most popular youth ministry resource. Every month, *Youthwork* is packed with resources, ideas and inspiration to help you in your work with young people. Each issue of *Youthwork* includes:

- an adaptable discussion starter

- four session plans, rooted in the Bible and tackling key themes for young people

- movie clips from the latest DVDs, applied for your work with youth

- drama sketches, designed for use in a range of contexts

- in-depth updates on developments in youth culture

- longer articles by the world's leading youth work writers

- reviews of the latest resources

- stories from on the ground youth workers

- plus news, interviews, regular columns and more!

To subscribe now, and receive a great free gift, visit www.youthwork.co.uk/subscribe